BEL
GRIFFITHS

MODERN SPIRITUAL MASTERS
Robert Ellsberg, Series Editor

This series introduces the writing and vision of some of the great spiritual masters of the twentieth century. Along with selections from their writings, each volume includes a comprehensive introduction, presenting the author's life and writings in context and drawing attention to points of special relevance to contemporary spirituality.

Some of these authors found a wide audience in their lifetimes. In other cases recognition has come long after their deaths. Some are rooted in long-established traditions of spirituality. Others charted new, untested paths. In each case, however, the authors in this series have engaged in a spiritual journey shaped by the influences and concerns of our age. Such concerns include the challenges of modern science, religious pluralism, secularism, and the quest for social justice.

At the dawn of a new millennium this series commends these modern spiritual masters, along with the saints and witnesses of previous centuries, as guides and companions to a new generation of seekers.

BEDE GRIFFITHS

Essential Writings

Selected with an Introduction by

THOMAS MATUS, OSB CAM

ORBIS BOOKS

Maryknoll, New York 10545

Copyright © 2004 by Orbis Books
Introduction © 2004 by Thomas Matus, OSB Cam

Published by Orbis Books, Maryknoll, NY 10545-0308.

Grateful acknowledgment is made to Templegate Publishers for permission to reprint excerpts from *The Golden String; The Marriage of East and West; Christ in India; A New Vision of Reality; Return to the Center; The New Creation in Christ; Cosmic Revelation; Universal Wisdom;* and *River of Compassion.* For permission to quote from *The New Creation in Christ* acknowledgment is also made to Darton, Longman and Todd Ltd. Excerpts from *Vedanta and Christian Faith* (The Dawn Press, 1973) reprinted by permission of the copyright owner, The Da Love-Ananda Samrajya Pty Ltd, as trustee for The Da Love-Ananda Samrajya. For all additional rights, thanks are due to the Bede Griffiths Trust.

The "Cosmic Cross," used here as an ornament, was devised by Bede Griffiths as a symbol for his community, Shantivanam. The inscription at the center is OM, the sacred word in the East from which all words arise. In Griffiths's words: "This means that we try to live our Benedictine Life in the context of Indian spirituality, that is, in the recognition of the Divine Presence in the whole cosmos and in the center of our own being."

Manufactured in the United States of America

Library of Congress Cataloging-in-Publication Data

Griffiths, Bede, 1906-
    [Selections. 2004]
    Bede Griffiths : essential writings / selected with an introduction by Thomas Matus.
    p. cm. – (Modern spiritual masters series)
    Includes bibliographical references.
    ISBN 1-57075-200-1 (pbk.)
    1. Christianity and other religions – Hinduism. 2. Hinduism – Relations – Christianity. 3. Griffiths, Bede, 1906- I. Matus, Thomas. II. Title. III. Series.
    BR128.H5 G68 2004
    261.2'45 – dc22

                                             2003019851

Contents

Introduction

Bede Griffiths, a Universal Monk

The more universal you become, the more deeply personal you become.

— BEDE GRIFFITHS, *The Cosmic Revelation*

Today, August 15, 1997, is the fiftieth birthday of modern India, the anniversary of her independence from the British crown. I write these lines in Rome, at the Monastery of Saint Gregory on the Cœlian Hill, from which, exactly fourteen centuries ago, Augustine, prior of this monastery, set out for Britain together with forty companions. In the south of England, at Canterbury, these Roman monks established a monastery and initiated the second evangelization of Britain.

Here at Saint Gregory's Monastery we Camaldolese Benedictines wear the white cowl. In England, too, there is a monastery of "white Benedictines": Prinknash Abbey, in Gloucestershire, of the congregation of Subiaco, where in 1933 Alan Griffiths, a fresh convert to the Catholic Church, put on the white cowl and was thereafter called Dom Bede. He went to India in 1955, assumed the garb and lifestyle of a *sannyasi* ("renunciant," as Hindus call their monks), and died in the South Indian state of Tamil Nadu, at the Ashram of Shantivanam, in 1993. The parabola of his life linked these places — India, Rome, and Britain, Subiaco and Camaldoli, Saint Gregory's Monastery and Shantivanam — like points on a star map, forming a strange constellation, and countless numbers of persons gravitated like wandering asteroids into his own far-ranging orbit, centered on God and on God's eternal Wisdom, which enters history "at many times and in many ways" (Heb. 1:1).

For those who wonder whether there was any symmetry between Bede's Roman Catholic monkhood and his Indian *sannyasa* ("renunciation"), let me summarize the story enfolded in his midlife autobiography, *The Golden String,* and spun out in his writings from India.*

Alan Griffiths was born in England on December 17, 1906, and was educated at a "public" school, Christ's Hospital, founded for gifted but poor youth; Samuel Coleridge, Charles Lamb, and the Benedictine mystic Dom Augustine Baker had their schooling there. In 1925 Alan "went up" to Magdalen College, Oxford, where he became the student and personal friend of the novelist C. S. Lewis. At first they did not directly discuss religious matters, but eventually they discovered they were both searching for a way out of the agnostic rationalism they had accepted as a provisional alternative to Christianity. In 1930, after leaving Oxford, Alan joined with two friends in leading a life of extreme simplicity in a Cotswold village, when he began to read the Bible and other Christian literature seriously. This "experiment in common life" led him to a new understanding of Christianity, and he returned to the sacraments in the Anglican Church. But he had not yet resolved his spiritual crisis; eventually he was received into the Catholic Church and became a Benedictine monk. At Prinknash Abbey he at last found peace and received the name Bede.

Being a monk and being a Christian were for Bede Griffiths the same thing. His vocation to "universality" came to him through Christ, but the Spirit was preparing him for another step, which would take him not "out of the Church" but in some way beyond its visible, canonical confines. He approached this further stage by a journey deep into the center of Benedictine mysticism. In 1954, the year before he left for India, Father

---

*In 1973, Bede penned a brief *curriculum vitae* as a preface to *Vedanta and Christian Faith* (Los Angeles: Dawn Horse Press, 1973), viii–ix.

Bede wrote of his experience of choral prayer and Eucharist at the Abbey of Prinknash:

> Time and space were obliterated, and we were gathered into that eternal present, in which all things stand in their essential unity before God. This was the center around which not only our own life but the life of the whole world moved. All the movements of the stars and atoms, the course of biological evolution and of human history, all derived their meaning from this. For Christ is the Head not only of all humankind but of the whole physical universe; all things, in Saint Paul's words, are to be gathered to a head in him. When he assumed a human nature, he assumed the whole universe in a certain sense into himself. For by the incarnation the whole universe is brought into organic relation with Christ and raised to a new mode of existence in him.... The creation was revealed for what it is, a symbol of the eternal reality manifested in time, a process of "becoming" always moving toward its realization in the order of absolute being, where each creature will participate according to its capacity in the divine glory.*

Bede Griffiths experienced the monastic choir as a bridge between the cosmos and the Absolute. At the same time, the training he received in the monastery revealed to him the double sense in which Christianity and the Church are and must become "catholic," that is, "according to the whole" (*kath'olon*) and "universal" (*katholike*). In general, Western thought finds the universal at the end of a process of analysis and abstraction; "universality" is a characteristic of a concept stripped of all concrete specificity and particularity. In the lived wisdom of monasticism, on the contrary, Bede Griffiths found himself becoming truly "catholic" and "universal" to the degree that he

---

*Bede Griffiths, *The Golden String* (London: Fount/HarperCollins, 1954, 1979), 162.

became grounded and centered in the concreteness of this specific community (the thirty holy but imperfect human beings he found at Prinknash when he joined) and of this specific practice of the spiritual life (the daily round of prayer, which made up the Divine Office, but also the manual labor and domestic tasks and fraternal recreation which occupied an equal amount of time in the abbey's daily schedule). So from the start, to be centered and grounded were for Father Bede synonyms for meditation and contemplative prayer.

Hence the monastic grounding of Bede Griffiths was the basis of his universalistic outlook, both of his sense of "cosmic redemption" and of his vision of the unity, the complementarity, and the differentiation of all religions. Father Bede was a Christian, and it was as such, unambiguously, that he presented himself when he engaged in dialogue with those of other faiths or of none. But then, as a monk, he discovered he was able to relate in a direct and concrete way with all religious persons, especially those belonging to traditions in which monasticism has played and plays a central role, such as Hinduism and Buddhism.

The first major office or "obedience" to which Father Bede was appointed after pronouncing his vows at Prinknash was that of guest master. In his Rule, Saint Benedict calls this officer the "Porter" and recommends that, as a senior member of the community, he be a wise man capable of giving good answers to the questions — expressed or tacit — of those who arrive at the monastery gates. It is not unlikely that at Monte Cassino Saint Benedict reserved this office for himself. As guest master of Prinknash, Bede Griffiths had the opportunity to meet and relate to persons "from all classes and professions and with all kinds of different religious backgrounds."* Thus he could bring to the fore and develop what was perhaps his principal charism beyond that of the monk: the ability to welcome,

---

*Ibid., 145–46.

listen to, and identify with the other, whatever might be the ethnic, cultural, or religious differences that stood between them. His ecumenism was exercised not only on an intellectual level (perhaps the only level apparent and of interest to his Western readers and disciples) but above all at the core of a shared spiritual experience.

It is only in prayer that we can communicate with one another at the deepest level of our being. Behind all words and gestures, behind all thoughts and feelings, there is an inner center of prayer where we can meet one another in the presence of God. It is this inner center which is the real source of all life and activity and of all love. If we could learn to live from that center we should be living from the heart of life, and our whole being would be moved by love. Here alone can all the conflicts of this life be resolved, and we can experience a love which is beyond time and change.*

Bede Griffiths authored a large number of books and articles, plus many unpublished manuscripts and taped conferences, which he left at his death. Much time and reflection will be necessary in order to evaluate their contribution to Christian theology and to cross-cultural studies in general. But all his readers have noted one characteristic of Bede Griffiths's thought: its continuity and inner consistency. In the closing chapters of his 1954 autobiography, *The Golden String,* he developed two themes — exemplified in the preceding quotations — to which he returned continually in the books and articles he authored during his Indian years (1955–93). The first was his vision of a cosmic revelation and redemption, to which he gained access through his participation in the daily rhythms of monastic prayer; the second was his way of meeting other religions and their adherents at the "inner center of prayer . . . in

---

*Ibid., 145.

the presence of God." It was there, at the heart of life, of being, and of love, "behind all words and gestures, behind all thoughts and feelings,... beyond time and change," that Bede Griffiths sought to understand the religions of India, their deepest and most universal meaning, that which they have in common with Christianity and those points in which they differ.

Bede Griffiths's Journey to India

The astronomical metaphor with which we began, stated in a slightly different way, can explain the relation of Bede Griffiths's midlife autobiography to the rest of his writings and his life. His orbit was like that of a comet, whose axis is the sun but whose parabola swings into a far aphelion. Bede left Prinknash Abbey for India in 1955, a year after publishing the story of his conversion to Catholicism and to the Benedictine monastic life. He made the journey with an Indian priest, Father Benedict Alapatt, who had professed monastic vows in a European abbey and desired to found a monastery in his native land. Bede's departure might have been read wrongly at the time, because in order to make the trip, he had to request an indult of exclaustration from the Holy See, a kind of suspension of part of his monastic vows. Someone might have judged this departure an admission of failure, if not a sign of personal inconsistency with the ideals he had held up to the public in his autobiography.

To the untrained eye, a comet arcing out of the solar system might seem lost in space. But the true stargazer knows that a parabolic arc always has its turning point, at which the comet, in obedience to the law of gravitation, resumes a centripetal movement. Bede saw a far galaxy — India, if you will — and embraced it in his orbit. But then he swung back, and the shape of his return was the mirror image of his departure.

Here is the metaphor done into conceptual categories: *The Golden String* is a perfect outline of Bede Griffiths's thought and work during the second half of his life. Every theme of this essay in autobiographical form can be found again and again in his subsequent essays, still subtly autobiographical. Change and development there were during his years in India, but his new ideas were always consistent with the wisdom he acquired before in his discovery of biblical revelation and monastic living. "The other half of my soul," which Bede sought and found in India, was as much an identical twin as a spouse of the Western half.

An early essay written in India stated some of the personal motives for his leaving the abbey in England:

> I had long been familiar with the mystical tradition of the West, but I felt the need of something more which the East alone could give; above all the sense of the presence of God in nature and the soul, a kind of natural mysticism which is the basis of all Indian spirituality. I felt therefore that if a genuine meeting of East and West was to take place, it must be at this deepest level of their experience, and this I thought could best come through the monastic life.*

Bede came to India with this holy desire, but he carried with him the cultural baggage of his nearly twenty-five years at Prinknash. Near Bangalore he and Father Alapatt built a small monastery in what they considered "simple" conditions, but Bede soon realized that their simplicity was luxury in comparison with the life of the local villagers, not to mention that of the Hindu ascetics, who begged their food and had no fixed abode.

The only solution, as Father Bede saw it, was *sannyasa*, total renunciation in conformity with the highest ideals of Indian asceticism. A few Catholic religious in those years had already arrived at this conclusion. In the South Indian state of Tamil Nadu, two French priests, Jules Monchanin and Henri

---

*Bede Griffiths, *Christ in India: Essays towards a Hindu-Christian Dialogue* (Springfield, Ill.: Templegate Publishers, 1965, 1984), 16.

Le Saux, a Benedictine, had been living as sannyasis in an *ashram* ("monastic dwelling, hermitage") they had dedicated to the Holy Trinity, using a Sanskrit term — *Saccidananda* — by which Hindus define the transcendent and immanent Absolute as "Being, Consciousness, Bliss." In 1958 a Belgian Trappist, Father Francis Mahieu, arrived at Saccidananda Ashram — also called *Shantivanam*, "Forest of Peace" — with his own ideas for a Christian monastic foundation. Father Francis contacted Bede Griffiths, who decided to leave Bangalore and join him in Kerala across the mountains. There they founded a cenobitic community, Trappist in observance but Indian in spirit. For their community prayer they adopted a Syrian liturgy in use among one of the ancient (perhaps even apostolic) Christian communities of southern India.

Father Monchanin soon died, and Father Le Saux, by then known as Swami Abhishiktananda, was uncertain whether he should continue the ashram experiment in the south or go north to the Himalayas, to live as a hermit among the Hindu sannyasis there. In 1968 he decided on the latter course and asked Father Mahieu to send some monks to take over Shantivanam. Father Bede came, together with two novices, Amaldas and Christudas, and Shantivanam began to assume the shape it has now.

The ashram is situated about twenty-five kilometers from the city of Tiruchirapalli (also called "Trichy"). You arrive there by the paved road in the direction of Kulittalai, until a sign in Tamil and English tells you to turn onto a dirt path that leads from the levees to the sacred river Kaveri, the "Ganges of the south." Through a polychromed arch with a three-faced figure (the Trinity as *Trimurti*, the divine triad sculpted into the rock of the Elephanta Caves) you enter a tree-shaded open space in front of the small temple, in perfect South Indian style. It is open to the tropical breezes; worshipers sit on the floor in a columned hall in front of the dark sanctuary, within whose obscure interior the tabernacle seems roughly the shape of the

Hindu *lingam*. The sanctuary is surmounted by a dome sustained by a lion, an ox, a bird, and a winged human figure — the same guardians you see at the corners of all the local temples, except that these are the four angelic creatures of the New Testament Apocalypse. This Indo-biblical symbolism was part of Father Monchanin's original project — blessed in 1950 by the far-seeing Indian bishop of Tiruchirapalli, Monsignor Mendonça — and Father Bede only completed the building of it, adding nearby another domed structure, which is the library. The rest of the grounds are occupied by the thatched-roof guest quarters, a few huts for those on solitary retreat, and the dining hall. Thick groves of coconut palms and flowering trees grace the whole with their fragrance and shade.

Bede Griffiths's twenty-five years at Shantivanam were quiet and focused. He dedicated his time and energies to meditation, the training of his Indian novices, and the welcoming of the guests — mostly from Europe and Australia, readers of his books — who filled the ashram's guest quarters from November to February, the most pleasant months in Tamil Nadu. In 1976 a young monk from the monastery of Camaldoli in Tuscany spent several months with him, and three years later Bede contacted our superiors and proposed the affiliation of Shantivanam with the thousand-year-old Holy Hermitage in the Apennines. Thus in 1980, thirty years after its founding, Saccidananda Ashram at Shantivanam became the Camaldolese "Hermitage of the Holy Trinity." Bede Griffiths knew the risk he was taking, connecting his ashram with a canonical monastic community close to Rome. He trusted my Italian brother and myself, who had lived with him and loved the ashram, to sustain his cause at Camaldoli. So far we have succeeded, and there is a reasonable hope that the ashram of the Christian sannyasis will arrive at its fiftieth anniversary as we enter Christendom's third millennium, intact in the unique form which Monchanin, Le Saux, and Griffiths gave it.

The Further Journeys of Bede Griffiths

Those who observed Bede Griffiths for any length of time at Shantivanam could see in him an example of monastic practice in which two disciplines were of the greatest importance — as they can be said to be the most important in the Rule of Saint Benedict: faithfulness to the times of common prayer and the hospitable reception of guests. With regard to the first, Father Bede had an almost mystical relationship to the bell that called the monks to prayer: for him it was simply the voice of God. All those who have spent more than a day at his ashram can remember how, at the first sound of the bell, he would calmly and mindfully set aside what he had at hand, drape his shawl over his bare shoulders, and walk with determined step the fifty meters from his hut to the temple. Like many tall men, he tended to bend forward slightly as he walked, but there was something else as well in this physical attitude: a gesture of eagerness, of expectancy, as of one heading toward an important event, a precious occasion in his life. If someone greeted him along the path, he would respond with a gentle smile and with the fewest necessary words, but then proceed to his place in the liturgical assembly.

This had been Father Bede's manner and attitude since he was a novice at Prinknash, when for the first time he heard what Saint Benedict considered to be a sign of a true vocation: if the novice "is truly seeking God, and if he is zealous for the work of God [the liturgical Hours], for obedience, and for humiliations." Of course what the Benedictine Rule calls "humiliations" are not those artificial mortifications invented by later spiritualities as tests of a candidate's mettle; for Saint Benedict they were nothing other than the novice's experience of his own limitations and those of his community, an experience which would teach him the monastic virtue of virtues, *discretio,* both "discretion" and "discernment."

The liturgical hours, tuned as they are to the cosmic rhythms of sunrise and sunset and the seasons of the year, already link the prayer of Christian monks to the religious and even mystical sense of the cosmos which is an essential characteristic of Hinduism. As for the structure and content of the liturgy at Shantivanam, Father Bede continued the practice instituted by Father Jules Monchanin. The ashram's first founder chose to take an Indian form of prayer and enrich it with elements of the Benedictine Office rather than attempt to "Indianize" the recitation of an existing breviary. However, Father Bede was concerned, as were Monchanin and Le Saux, to keep the liturgical inculturation practiced at Shantivanam safely within the limits approved by the local bishops and the Holy See. Hence the Hindu, Buddhist, Sikh, and Sufi texts, read at the beginning of each Hour, are seen clearly as a preparation for the Christian prayer, which opens with the sign of the cross and the invocation of the Holy Trinity.

Although Bede Griffiths was a man of vast culture and refined tastes, accustomed to the Gregorian chant he had known and loved at his abbey in England, he never complained about the poor quality of some of the Christian *bhajan* songs or of the brothers' voices. He preferred, with great discretion, to inculcate in them by example a spirit of prayer and of enthusiastic participation in the liturgy. I remember well how Father Bede enjoyed following the rhythm of the Indian chants, beating time on a small drum.

Father Bede's role at Shantivanam was officially that of monastic superior; in his own intention it was that of "teacher" (*acharya* or *guru*); but in its widest-ranging effect it remained that of guest master, the wise elder who welcomes the pilgrim without asking any questions, in love and in prayer, seeing him or her "as Christ himself."* Father Bede never enjoyed a moment of privacy at the ashram. His windows were always open, and his door was shut only at night. But even then, one of the Indian brothers or workers would sleep on the verandah

---

*Cf. Rule of Saint Benedict 53,1.7.

or keep watch near by. When Father Bede received someone, he invariably gave that person the impression of being at the center of his attention, as if, at that moment, she were the only person in the world for him. He was an excellent listener and knew how to help others express their own thoughts and feelings. If one asked a question, he would answer it simply and briefly, and if the question regarded his own person, he would try to change the subject or else offer the questioner a copy of one of his books, saying that the answer was there.

In an account of a brief stay at Shantivanam in 1980, the Trappist writer Basil Pennington remarked ironically that among the guests in the ashram at that moment, the only Asian was Father John Bosco Kim, a Benedictine from Korea. While it is true that during the 1970s most of the "pilgrims" to Shanti-vanam were from Europe, North America, and Australia, after the incorporation of the ashram into the Camaldolese Benedictine congregation, and with more favorable attitudes toward incul-turation and the interreligious dialogue among India's Catholics, the vast majority came to be Indians; for the most part these were Christians, but there was also an occasional Hindu, Buddhist, or Parsee. During the month immediately following Father Bede's death, the several dozen guests — the Jesuit novices of Tamil Nadu, a community of sisters, numerous lay persons — included only four or five non-Indians.

Whether we see Bede Griffiths as the contemplative monk, always mindful and always ready, at the first sound of the bell, to proceed to his place in church for the choral prayer, or as the gentle master of guests, the attentive listener and man of wisdom, we must recognize in him above all the mark of the prophet, of one whose very existence as a Catholic monk in India proclaimed and evoked that "wholeness" and that "universality" which are intrinsic to the notion of catholicity and which must become the distinctive marks of the Church in India.

Bede Griffiths's final years were filled with writing and world travels. In 1990 he had a stroke, but as he was slowly recovering his mobility and strength, his elder disciple Amaldas succumbed to a heart attack and died at the age of forty-two. At that moment, something like a miracle took place. Father Bede rose from his sickbed with a new sense of mission. Half of that year and of the two following he traveled abroad, visiting groups of laypeople who had gathered to read his books, had perhaps come all the way to India to meet him, but above all were seeking a way of meditation that would introduce the contemplative experience into their everyday existence.

Father Bede felt drawn to promote the network of "Christian meditation centers" initiated by the late John Main, a fellow Benedictine, whom Bede had met in 1979 and who had died in 1982. A "John Main Seminar" held in 1991 at a conference center in the United States had Bede Griffiths as its chief speaker, and his lectures and conversations became a book, *The New Creation in Christ*, which offers the clearest statement of his thought on Christian spirituality in dialogue with the spiritualities of the East. The fall of 1992 brought him to England and continental Europe. In September he made his last visit to Camaldoli, where he put on the white Benedictine cowl for the last time and joined in blessing the monastic profession of two Italian novices.

Radiant with joy for having reconnected with his own monastic novitiate, Bede Griffiths returned to Shantivanam, where a second stroke, and then a third, left him paralyzed on the left side of his body. His mind, however, remained clear, and he could still speak, although with difficulty. But the stroke had completely robbed him of his sense of time and space. No longer was he sure when or where he was — in fact, as those who assisted him realized, he was already in eternity. The last five months were a Gethsemani experience, an "agony in the garden" for both guru and disciples.

"Living in Unity"

"What can we do?" asked Father Bede. Around his hut at Shantivanam there was perfect silence, not even the stirring of a breeze in the palm fronds. It was about 11 p.m. on April 26, 1993, and Brother Martin would be assisting his dying guru until around three in the morning, when Father Christudas would come to take his place.

To his teacher's question, Brother Martin replied, "You have to impart your grace to me."

Father Bede's next words had that surreal quality common to most of his nighttime conversations during these months since his third stroke: "I am waiting to come live here with you. I think I can honestly say that."

"We will be very happy to have you here with us," said Brother Martin.

"And what about Christudas?" asked Father Bede.

"He will be with us."

"And Amaldas?"

"Amaldas also."

Father Bede, reassured, pointed to his desk. "Now, would you put that down in writing? That is what I really want."

"What do you want?" asked Martin.

Father Bede replied, "I really want you and Christudas and Amaldas and me to be living as brothers in unity. That is what 'grace' is in my life. Can we do that?"

"Yes, we can do that," said Brother Martin.

During the five, long months of his final illness — his "agony in the garden" — Bede Griffiths repeatedly expressed his concern for the small monastic community of seven Indian brothers at Shantivanam. The future of this fragile community nucleus was his great obsession as death approached and his physical and mental faculties were failing.

"My monastery is the world," Bede Griffiths had often said; yet he knew well that the universality of the Benedictine ideal is fulfilled in the specificity of *this* concrete monastery and *this* concrete group of brothers — with all their "physical and moral defects," writes Saint Benedict in his Rule. As "guru" (Father Bede did not like to be called by this title), there was no one to succeed him. His only successor, his legacy and his testament, were to be the brothers themselves, living by that grace of unity of which — he remembered as he lay dying — he had sung so many times in the monastic choir of Prinknash Abbey. As the antiphon to the Vulgate Psalm 132 at Tuesday Vespers says: *Ecce quam bonum et quam jucundum habitare fratres in unum,* "How good and pleasant it is, to live as brothers in unity."

On Saturday, May 8, six days before his death, Father Bede was assisted by Sister Marie-Louise, a Benedictine who has an ashram for women next to Shantivanam. At sunrise, just before Mass, Father Bede suddenly said, in a loud voice, "I must go to the Camaldolese!"

"But Father," she said, "that is in Italy; it is very far to travel."

Father Bede insisted. "Marie-Louise, hurry up! I must go to the Camaldolese. They are waiting for me."

After he had repeated this a third time, Marie-Louise said, clearly and gently, "Father, arrangements have to be made. The flight has to be booked, and Christudas has to go to Trichy to do the booking."

"No, that is all too late," he said. "I must go just now. I don't need the booking. The car is here; I want to go by car."

So Marie-Louise had the brothers lift Father Bede into his wheelchair and took him to the temple at the entrance to the ashram. But as she wheeled him toward his usual place in the temple, he said, "Why have you brought me here? I have resigned from this place. I must go to the Camaldolese."

The days that followed saw Father Bede, seized with a violent fever, moving in and out of consciousness, only now and then recognizing those who saw to his needs. At the last anointing he opened his eyes and resumed the invocations that were

on his lips during the final hours: the prayer of the Russian pilgrim ("Lord Jesus Christ, Son of God, have mercy on me" —
he would pause — "a sinner") and "Alleluia, alleluia, alleluia,"
repeated many times.

On May 12, the eve of his death, having received the anointing of the sick, Bede Griffiths expressed his last desire. "Will
you help me?" he said.

Christudas replied, "We are here to help you, my dear."

Father Bede said, "Let me die in the church. Just as Saint
Benedict: they held him in his place in choir... they held him
in choir, in choir — help me." His voice was so faint that
those around him could not make out his words. But a cas-
sette recorder was on nearby, and as I listened to the tape a few
days after his burial, I recognized Father Bede's allusion to the
story of Saint Benedict's death in Saint Gregory the Great's second book of *Dialogues*: the dying patriarch asked his monks to
carry him into the oratory to receive Holy Communion, and as
they held his arms aloft in prayer, he breathed his last.

This was not to be the precise manner of Bede Griffiths's
passing; he was to remain a victim on the altar of his sickbed.
But in his final intention he had indeed "returned to the center,"
to the place of his deepest experiences of prayer as a Christian.

The year in which Bede Griffiths concluded his life's journey, 1993, also marked the twenty-fifth anniversary of the death
of Thomas Merton, another monk and man of letters, who
sought to penetrate, by means of a contemplative connatural-
ity, into the depths of Asian religions. But whereas Merton, in
his published and unpublished works, arrived at a succession
of turning-points where he reexamined and significantly modi-
fied his judgments and perspectives, Griffiths's thought evolved
gradually, as the Catholic Church and its theology have evolved,
but he kept the golden string in hand.

Bede Griffiths never let drop that golden string, and it did indeed — as in William Blake's poem — lead him in at heaven's
gate. But there he found that Jerusalem's wall had fallen. The

Church itself, at the Second Vatican Council, had taken to heart the words of Saint Paul to the Ephesians (2:14) and had allowed its defensive ramparts to be broken through from within by the force of Christ's own love, so that all hostility between the Church and the other religions might cease, and relations of peace, understanding, and love might prevail among them.

•

A note on Father Bede's use of "man" and "men": like all writers of his epoch he came upon the problem of inclusive language late in his career as an author. I have found, however, that "genderism" is less apparent in his earlier writings than in those of, for example, Thomas Merton. Having lived through the 1970s, Father Bede came to recognize the need of inclusive language (at least on the "horizontal" plane, when speaking of human beings and their relationships), and he ordered those who transcribed and edited his recorded lectures and his writings to introduce a consistently inclusive style into them. I have followed these indications in the excerpts chosen from his earlier writings and have substituted terms like "human beings" or "humankind" where "men" or "mankind" appeared in the original edition of the text.

1

A Vision of Nature

Bede Griffiths's first book was published in 1954, when he was nearly forty-eight years old. The Golden String *told the story of his spiritual pilgrimage, culminating in his conversion to Roman Catholicism and his almost simultaneous entry into monastic life at the abbey of Prinknash in the Cotswolds. The first passage in this anthology is the opening page of the autobiography, a prose poem which tells of an experience which many teenagers might have had but which few have later described in such vivid terms.*

Through the tinted lens of his quasi-mystical vision of nature, the mature Bede Griffiths closely examined both classical Hindu orthodoxy and the mechanistic scientific paradigm with its technological and industrial fallout, and found both wanting. In Hinduism, a certain popular interpretation of the Upanishads' nondualism saw the world, the stars, the earth, living creatures, and each individual soul as maya, *pure illusion. Father Bede, committed to the dialogue with Hinduism as few others before him, criticized this interpretation, especially for its consequences in the social psychology of the Indian people — their resignation to destiny, their tendency to withdraw from earthly realities, even their sense of superiority to "worldly" Westerners. However, he recognized that this popular mentality did not represent the authentic thought of the Upanishads, and he even suggested that the doctrine of Shankara, the great Hindu doctor of non-dualism, was not far from the teaching of Thomas Aquinas on contingent being, the created world, as existing not of itself but only in relation to the one absolute Being, God.*

As for scientific thought, Bede Griffiths distinguished between the traditional mechanistic paradigm, on which the edifice of industrial society is based, and the newer vision of reality, the "network" model propounded by such thinkers as David Bohm, Rupert Sheldrake, and Fritjof Capra. The metaphor of the universe as a complex web of interdependent relationships enabled the scientist to think of the universe as a whole, with many hidden dimensions, and not just as an assemblage of parts, which could be examined separately and then exploited without concern for their place in the whole.

Bede's teenage vision of nature as the thinly veiled "face of God" came back to him several times throughout his life. A second experience, almost as powerful as the first, was occasioned by a visit to Prinknash as he was completing his passage to Catholicism. This time he discovered a different kind of beauty, one which radiates from within the human soul as she prays and contemplates the mystery of grace. He discovered the supernatural connection between the physical cosmos and the sacramental cosmos of Christian faith, and the universe became for him a sacrament of the mystery of death and resurrection.

The vision came to him again in India, more than once. He saw "sacred nature" through the contemplative gaze of the sages and artists who had left their testimony — the divine Triad — carved into the rock of the Elephanta Caves off the coast of Bombay (India's great port city, now called Mumbai). Finally, half a century after his playing-field vision (described on the following page), he once more saw the same light of the setting sun, heard the same bird songs and the same voice of the soft wind in the trees, and smelled the same fragrances, but now he was in India, at the ashram he had inherited from Monchanin and Le Saux, by the banks of the river Kaveri. He saw nature in its beauty and in its fragile contingency, and above all he saw his own contingent being both within the cosmic body of the universe and within the Word, the ground of nature, in which he had existed from all eternity.

SUNSET IN SUSSEX

I give you the end of a golden string;
Only wind it into a ball,
It will lead you in at heaven's gate,
Built in Jerusalem's wall.

— WILLIAM BLAKE

One day during my last term at school I walked out alone in the evening and heard the birds singing in that full chorus of song which can only be heard at that time of the year at dawn or at sunset. I remember now the shock of surprise with which the sound broke on my ears. It seemed to me that I had never heard the birds singing before, and I wondered whether they sang like this all year round and I had never noticed it. As I walked on I came upon some hawthorn trees in full bloom, and again I thought that I had never seen such a sight or experienced such sweetness before. If I had been brought suddenly among the trees of the Garden of Paradise and heard a choir of angels singing I could not have been more surprised. I came then to where the sun was setting over the playing fields. A lark rose suddenly from the ground beside the tree where I was standing and poured out its song above my head, and then sank still singing to rest. Everything then grew still as the sunset faded and the veil of dusk began to cover the earth. I remember now the feeling of awe which came over me. I felt inclined to kneel on the ground, as though I had been standing in the presence of an angel; and I hardly dared to look on the face of the sky, because it seemed as though it was but a veil before the face of God.

These are the words with which I tried many years later to express what I had experienced that evening, but no words can do more than suggest what it meant to me. It came to me quite suddenly, as it were out of the blue, and now that I look back on it, it seems to me that it was one of the decisive events of my life. Up to that time I had lived the life of a normal schoolboy, quite content with the world as I found it. Now I was suddenly made aware of another world of beauty and mystery such as I had never imagined to exist, except in poetry. It was as though I had begun to see and smell and hear for the first time. The world appeared to me as Wordsworth describes it with "the glory and freshness of a dream." The sight of a wild rose growing on a hedge, the scent of lime tree blossoms caught suddenly as I rode down a hill on a bicycle, came to me like visitations from another world. But it was not only that my senses were awakened. I experienced an overwhelming emotion in the presence of nature, especially at evening. It began to wear a kind of sacramental character for me. I approached it with a sense of almost religious awe, and in the hush which comes before sunset, I felt again the presence of an unfathomable mystery. The song of the birds, the shapes of the trees, the colors of the sunset, were so many signs of this presence, which seemed to be drawing me to itself.[1]

AT PRINKNASH ABBEY

I had often driven out to the old Cistercian abbey of Hailes near Winchcombe when I was at Oxford, and I had visited Rievaulx and Fountains and other medieval ruins; but they were simply relics of the past to me, and I had no idea that there were any existing in the modern world. The discovery, therefore, that there was a monastery actually within a few miles of Gloucester and Cheltenham came as a complete surprise. But as soon as I came there I knew that this was what I had unconsciously been seeking all these years. Even now after twenty years I can recall the impression which it first made on me. It was an experience almost as surprising as my first discovery of the beauty of nature at school.

The natural setting was certainly as lovely as could be imagined. It was an old Cotswold manor house standing on the side of a hill, where the Cotswolds slope down to meet the plain. The country had none of the bare austerity of the hills above Northleach with their grim gray walls running across the windswept fields. Here the fields were studded with trees like a park. In front lay the plain stretching to the Malvern hills in the distance, and the tower of what had once been Gloucester Abbey rising up in the foreground as a silent witness to the religion which had once dominated the countryside.

It was not, however, the outward setting which now moved me. I discovered what had been the inner life of the cathedrals and monasteries which I had visited in the past. It was a beauty of a different kind from anything which I had known before, a beauty not of the natural but of the supernatural order. The presence of God had been revealed to me on that day at school beneath the forms of nature, the birds' song, the flowers' scent, the sunset over the fields; but now it was another presence which I perceived, the presence of God in the mystery not of nature but of Grace. Externally it was shown in the white habits of the monks, in the chant and ceremonies of the choir, in the order and dignity of the life which they led, and it was not long before I discovered the inner secret of the life. It was something which had been hidden from me all these years, something which I had been seeking without knowing exactly what it was, the secret of prayer.

Prayer had always been for me something private and apart, something of which one would never dream of speaking to anyone else. But now I found myself in an atmosphere where prayer was the breath of life. It was accepted as something as normal as eating and drinking. . . . I realized now what it was that I had missed all this time. It was the absence of prayer as a permanent background to life which made modern life so empty and meaningless. Life in the modern world was cut off from its source in God; people's minds were shut up in the confines of the material world and their own personalities, unable to escape from their fetters. Here the mind was kept open to God, and everything was brought into relation with him.[2]

THE UNIVERSE AS SACRAMENT

The human imagination has always been haunted by the feeling that we must die in order that we may live; that we have to be born again. To be a Christian is to accept this mystery of death and resurrection in one's own life; it is to pass through the world of appearances into the realm of Being. It is to commit oneself to the view that the world as we know it is not the world for which we are created. It is to confess that we are "strangers and exiles on earth"; that we have here "no abiding city." Already science has begun to recognize that the outward forms of matter, the molecules and atoms, the protons and electrons with which it deals, are only a kind of algebra, a symbolic representation of certain elemental powers whose real nature we do not know. We know that we ourselves, and the whole universe of which we are a part, are in a state of evolution, passing continually from one state of being to another. Everything is subject to the same law of transformation.

But what is the end of this process? Of this science can tell us nothing, but divine revelation comes to our aid. It tells us that the whole of this world of space and time is destined to pass away; there is to be "a new heaven and a new earth," where "time will be no more." We are to be reunited in a new order of Being, a society transcending the limitations of this world, in which we will participate in the life of God. We are to enter into the vision of God, that vision of all things in their eternal truth, which is the object of all our quest on earth.[3]

The whole universe is a sacrament, which mirrors the divine reality; . . . each created thing, though nothing in itself, is of infinite value and significance, because it is the sign of a mystery which is enshrined in the depths of its being. . . . Every human being is . . . not merely an isolated individual carried along on the flux of time and doomed to extinction, but a member of a divine society, working out its destiny in space and time and subject to all the tragic consequences of subservience to the material world, but destined to transcend the limitations of time and space and mortality, and to enter into that fullness of life where there shall be "neither mourning nor weeping nor pain any more." The suffering of this world can have no meaning as long as we attempt to judge it in the light of this present time. We are like people who hear snatches of music, which they have no means of relating to the symphony as a whole. But when we have passed beyond the conditions of this present life we shall then have that integral knowledge in which the whole is known in every part, and every part is seen to mirror the whole.[4]

THE PERPETUAL ALLEGORY

In the Paleolithic caves which have been discovered in the south of France it has been found that there are long winding passages leading from the front of the cave by a difficult and often dangerous path into the inmost recesses of the rock, and there in the darkness of the interior are to be found those drawings of animals which astonish us with their power and beauty. Why was it that these pictures were drawn in the darkness of the interior where they could only be seen by the light of a torch of moss dipped in animal fat? Miss Rachel Levy in her *Gate of Horn* has given us the answer. The pictures on the wall were the sacred images by means of which it was believed that human beings could enter into communion with the divine powers, and the long, winding, difficult passage to the interior represented the dark and difficult approach to the divine mystery.

We find this symbolism continued all through Neolithic times, in the megalithic temples and in the ritual dances of primitive peoples today; always there is the laborious approach to the sacred place where the encounter with the divine mystery is to take place.... Thus from the earliest times of which we have any knowledge, it seems to have been understood that our life in this world is a journey toward God. The journey is from the mouth of the cave, which represents the external world, into the interior which appears as darkness; it is the passage from the outer to the inner world. It is this journey which is represented by the descent of Aeneas into the underworld in search of his father. The same motive appears in the Odyssey as the return of the Hero by a long and difficult voyage home, where his wife awaits him. Or again it is found in the legend of Theseus making his way to the center of the Labyrinth in search of his Bride.

All these stories are symbols of the same mystery of the search for God which is at the same time the return to our true home. It is represented sometimes as a new birth, a return to the womb, or again as a descent into the tomb by which we rise again to a new life. Always it has been understood that our life in this world, as Keats said, is a "perpetual allegory"; everything has meaning only in reference to something beyond. We are, as Plato saw it, like persons in a cave who see reality reflected on the walls of the cave, as in a cinema. The illusion of this world is that by which we mistake the figures on the screen for reality. This is the sin of idolatry, for idolatry is nothing but the worship of images, the mistaking the image of truth for Truth itself.

Scientific materialism in the modern world is the precise counterpart of pagan idolatry in the ancient world; it is the substitution of appearance for reality. For science as such is only concerned with phenomena, that is, with things as they appear to the senses: its function is, in the Greek phrase, to "save the phenomena," to account for the appearance of things. But of the reality which underlies the appearance, of the real nature of things, science can give us no knowledge at all. We only begin to awake to reality when we realize that the material world, the world of space and time, as it appears to our senses, is nothing but a sign and a symbol of a mystery which infinitely transcends it. That is why the images in the Paleolithic caves were painted in the dark; it is only when we have passed beyond the world of images that we can enter into communion with the mystery which lies beyond.

This sense of a mystery transcending the world, of which this world, as we know it, is only a sign, is the root of all religion. It underlies the religion of primitive humanity; it is embodied in the ancient myths and legends; it is found at the basis both of Egyptian and Babylonian religion, and it takes shape finally in the mystery religions which are found all over the ancient world. In these religions the cycle of life and death in nature, the passage of the seasons through the death of winter to rebirth in the spring, is seen as a symbol of our passage through death into life, of our rebirth to immortality.

In the great awakening which took place in so many different parts of the world in the first millennium before Christ, which Karl Jaspers called the "axial period" of human history, the full significance of this religion comes to light. It was then that as by a kind of universal awakening the real meaning of life seems to have dawned upon the human mind. In India and China, in Persia and in Greece, a movement of thought began, by which humanity finally pierced through the barrier of the senses and discovered the mystery of the world which lies beyond. This was the great discovery which brought enlightenment to the Buddha; this was the source of the inspiration of the Upanishads and the tradition of the Vedanta: this was what was revealed in China as the Tao and in Greece as the Logos.

To each people the mystery was revealed in a different way. To the Indian it came rather as sense of the utter unreality of the phenomenal world in comparison with the reality of that which lay beyond. To the Chinese it appeared as a principle of harmony, a cosmic order uniting humankind and nature in an organic society. The Greek saw it as a law of Reason by which "all things are steered through all things," which gave rise to Plato's conception of the "world of ideas" and to Plotinus's vision of the One, transcending all thought and all being.[5]

THE TRUTH OF THE IMAGINATION

Since my coming to India, I have been led in a strange way to retrace the path of the Golden String. My awakening to the mystery of existence had come to me through the experience of the beauty of nature, which I have described in the opening chapter of *The Golden String,* and this experience had been expressed and interpreted for me in the writings of the Romantic poets, Wordsworth, Shelley, and Keats. Wordsworth had taught me to find in nature the presence of a power which pervades both the universe and the human mind.... Shelley had awakened me to the Platonic idea of an eternal world, of which the world we see is a dim reflection. Keats had set before me the values of "the holiness of the heart's affections and the truth of the imagination." These were for me not merely abstract ideas but living principles, which were working in me over many years and which I tried to comprehend in a reasoned philosophy of life.

But when I came to India, these ideas took on a new life. I discovered that what in Europe had been the inspired intuition of a few poets had been the common faith of India for countless centuries. That power which pervades the universe and the mind . . . had been revealed with marvelous insight in the Vedas [fifteen] centuries before the birth of Christ. The eternal world of Plato was only a reflection in the Western mind of the profound intuition of the seers of the Upanishads [1000–500 B.C.E.]. Above all, I found that "the truth of the imagination," of which Keats had spoken, was a primordial truth, a truth which takes us back to the very roots of human experience. The Western mind from the time of Socrates and Plato had concentrated on the development of abstract, rational thought which had led to the great systems of theology in the Middle Ages and to the achievements of modern science and philosophy. But India had been nourished from the beginning by the truth of the imagination, the primordial truth, which is not abstract but concrete, not logical but symbolic, not rational but intuitive. So it was that I was led to the rediscovery of the truth which the Western world had lost and is now desperately seeking to recover.[6]

SACRED NATURE

When I first landed at Bombay I went to see the Elephanta Caves, and the great statue of Shiva there left a lasting impression on me. Here at the threshold of India I found graven in stone that profound spirit of contemplation which has given its inner meaning to all Indian life and thought. It is recollected in a deep repose, like so many statues of the Buddha, revealing in stone that awareness of the inner Spirit, the Atman, which to the Hindu is the ground of all existence. When I went on to visit the temples of Mysore and later of Tamil Nadu, I discovered how the whole Hindu temple is a shrine of this inner

Spirit. The outer walls may be decorated with figures of animals and human beings and gods, so that one is led by stages
through the different levels of life in this world, but in the central shrine — the *garbha griha,* representing the "cave of the
heart" — there may be nothing but a *lingam,* a bare stone representing the formless divinity, the absolute Godhead which is
beyond all "name and form."

The sexual origin of the *lingam* is, of course, obvious, but
this only brings out the extraordinary depth of understanding of
ancient India. Sex was always regarded as something "holy" —
I think it still is, except where the Indian spirit has been cor-
rupted by the West. The *lingam* was therefore a natural symbol
of the sacred "source of life." But with the profound metaphysical sense of ancient India this source of life was inevitably seen
not as a mere biological reality but as the absolute Being, the
eternal reality which is life and consciousness and bliss....

Perhaps this is the deepest impression left by life in India,
the sense of the sacred as something pervading the whole order
of nature. Every hill and tree and river is holy, and the sim-
plest human acts of eating and drinking, still more of birth and
marriage, have all retained their sacred character. It is this that
gives such an indescribable beauty to Indian life, in spite of the
poverty and squalor....

This Hindu sense of the sacred was wonderfully illustrated
for me one day when I was living near Bangalore. I was visiting a little temple to the monkey-god Hanuman, the faithful
companion of Rama in the story of the Ramayana, which was a
short distance from our monastery. As I was coming away I met
an old Brahmin, who spoke good English and had, in fact, been
educated in a Christian school. He no doubt wondered what
I would make of a monkey-god and began to explain to me
that God is manifested in every form in the universe, whether
in plant or animal or human being; it is therefore possible to
worship God, the one infinite, eternal Being, under the form of
a monkey, as in that of a tree or a human being. But above

all, he went on to say, God is present in the human heart, and he quoted some stanzas of the Bhagavad Gita in Sanskrit in the rhythmical chant which is used in the recitation of Sanskrit. This was a wonderful example to me of the deep roots of Hindu tradition, the sense of the one eternal Spirit pervading the universe and manifested in everything, which has been enshrined in the doctrine of the Upanishads and the Bhagavad Gita, and come down into the life of the ordinary villager today. In this sense it is difficult to speak of either polytheism or idolatry in Hinduism; for to the Hindu every god is but a manifestation of the one, eternal absolute Being, and every idol is but the sacramental presence of the one infinite Spirit.[7]

TEMPLES, HUMAN AND COSMIC

[While living near Bangalore,] I was studying Sanskrit with Raimundo Panikkar, who embodies in a unique way this meeting of East and West. His mother was a Spanish Catholic, and his father came from a well-known Hindu family. He had been brought up in Europe, had taken degrees in science, philosophy, and theology, and had now come to India to discover his Indian heritage. Together we explored this Indian culture which was now beginning to unfold before my eyes. We spent some weeks together visiting the temples in the old Mysore State.

At the very beginning there was an unforgettable experience, when . . . a man whom we met on the way [invited us] to visit his home. He took us to a tiny, two-roomed cottage, where we sat cross-legged on the floor, and two little boys gave us a concert of Indian classical music. There was no furniture in the house. One little boy was lying ill on a mat on the floor, and the others sat beside us, one playing a stringed instrument, and both singing together, beating the time with their hands and completely absorbed in the music. The mother prepared tea in the kitchen, which we drank from small brass vessels, but later she too came and played and sang herself. The father explained to us the meaning of the songs, which were either in Sanskrit or one of the South Indian languages, and were all, of course, religious. So there we were sitting on the floor in this little cottage with no modern conveniences, brought face to face with one of the most profound religious cultures of the world.

Our visits to the temples only confirmed this impression. At Belur, Halebid, and Somnathpur we found architecture and sculpture of a beauty and refinement equal to the finest Gothic art, but beyond the outward form of beauty there was the deep, inner meaning of the temples.

Halebid in particular was a most enchanting place, an old temple set in a lovely valley with a broad river flowing by, reminding one of [the ruins of] Tintern or Fountains [in England]. Round the outside of the temple there are sculptured friezes in ascending order, representing first the animal world — elephants, horses, birds — then the human world with stories from the Hindu epics, the *Ramayana* and the *Mahabharata,* and finally the divine world, the world of the gods and goddesses. It was a manifestation of the cosmic mystery in stone, the divine life manifesting itself in the three worlds, the animal, the human, and the divine.

Another impression of lasting significance was the figure of a naked man standing upright, to be found in many of the Jain temples here, above all the colossal figure in the temple at Sravana Belgola. This, I believe, is the figure of Purusha, the Primeval Man, the Archetypal Man, who appears in the Rig Veda, of whom it is said that he contains the whole creation in himself. "Three-quarters of him is above in heaven, one-quarter is here on earth." This is akin to the Adam Kadmon, the first Adam, of Jewish tradition, and [to] the Universal Man of Muslim tradition. When Jesus called himself the Son of Man, he was relating himself to this primeval tradition and revealing the underlying unity of religions. Thus the temples in Mysore revealed

Hinduism as the cosmic religion, the religion of God's revelation in the cosmos and in humankind....

It is this vision of a cosmic unity, in which human beings and nature are sustained by an all-pervading spirit, which the West needs to learn from the East. It is this that explains the extraordinary sacredness which attaches to every created thing in India. The earth is sacred, and no plowing or sowing or reaping can take place without some religious rite. Eating is a sacred action, and every meal is conceived as a sacrifice to God. Water is sacred, and no religious Hindu will take a bath without invoking the sacred power of the water, which descends from heaven and, caught on the head of Shiva, is distributed in the fertilizing streams of the Ganges and other rivers. Air is sacred, the breath of life which comes from God and sustains all living creatures. Fire is sacred, especially in its source in the sun, which brings light and life to all creatures. So also with plants and trees, especially certain plants like the tulsi plant and certain trees like the banyan. Animals are sacred, especially the cow, which gives her milk as a mother, but also the elephant, the monkey, and the snake. Finally, the human person is sacred, ... a manifestation of God, but especially a holy person, in whom the divine presence can be more clearly seen.

This is the sacred universe, in which humanity has lived as far as we know from the beginning of history, and which has been completely demolished by the Western, scientific world. Every trace of sacredness has been removed from life, so that "Western man" finds himself in a universe in which both human existence and nature have been deprived of any ultimate meaning.[8]

SUNSET AT SHANTIVANAM

I sit here on the verandah of my cell [at Saccidananda Ashram, Shantivanam], watching the sun set behind the trees, and I recall the day, nearly fifty years ago, when I watched the same sun setting over the playing-fields at school. My cell is a thatched hut surrounded by trees. I can listen to the birds singing, as I did then, and watch the trees making dark patterns against the sky as the light fades, but I have traveled a long way both in space and in time since then. There are tall palmyra palms around me, and young coconut trees growing up between them, and the bananas are spreading their broad leaves like green sails. I can hear a robin singing, but it is a black Indian robin, and the voice of the cuckoo which comes from the distant woods is that of the Indian cuckoo. I have made my home here in India, in the Tamil Nadu, by the banks of the river Kaveri, but my mind has also traveled no less far than my body. For sixteen years now I have lived as an Indian among Indians, following Indian ways of life, studying Indian thought, and immersing myself in the living traditions of the Indian spirit. Let me now try to reflect on what India has done to me, on how my mind has developed over these years, on the changes which have taken place in my way of life and in the depths of my soul.

The first thing I have learned is a simplicity of life which before I would not have thought possible. India has a way of reducing human needs to a minimum. One full meal a day of rice and vegetables — at best with some curds and ghee (clarified butter) — is considered sufficient. Tea or coffee with some rice preparation and some pickle is enough for breakfast and supper. Nor are tables and chairs, spoons and forks and knives and plates considered necessary. One sits on the floor on a mat and eats with one's hands — or rather with the right hand, as the left hand is kept for cleansing one's self. For a plate there is a banana leaf. There is thus no need of any furniture in an Indian home. The richer people who have adopted Western ways may make use of tables and chairs and beds and other conveniences, but the poor person — and that is the vast majority — is still content to sit and sleep on the floor. Nor are elaborate bathrooms and lavatories considered necessary. In the villages the majority of people will take their bath at a pump or a well or in a neighboring tank or stream, and most people still go out into the fields or by the roadside or by a stream to relieve themselves. There is a beautiful simplicity in all this, which makes one realize something of the original simplicity of human nature. Even clothes are hardly necessary. Most men today, it is true, wear a shirt and a *dhoti* — a piece of cloth wound round the waist and falling to the feet — and women wear a sari and a blouse to cover the breast, but this is comparatively recent. Even now clothes are still felt to be things which are put on for the occasion, and are easily discarded. A man will take his shirt off when he wants to relax, and a laborer will wear no more than a *langothi* — a piece of cloth wound round the middle and between the legs.

All this makes the life of the sannyasi — one who has "renounced" the world — immensely simple. Sannyasis need no house or furniture. They may live in a cave or take shelter beside a temple or on the verandah of a house. For clothing they need only two pieces of cloth — which should not be stitched — one to wear around the waist and the other for a shawl to cover the shoulders or the head. There are even some sannyasis who renounce all clothing and are said to be "clothed with the sky." For food they need only one meal a day, which they get by begging or, more often, which a householder will offer them unasked. They can thus reduce their life to an absolute simplicity. They are totally detached from the world, depending on divine providence for their bare needs of food, shelter, and clothing. Does this not bring them very near to the first disciples of Christ, who were told to take "no gold, nor silver, nor copper in your belts, no bag for your journey, nor two tunics, nor sandals, nor a staff," and to the Son of Man himself, who had nowhere to lay his head? What a challenge this presents to a world which takes pleasure in continually increasing human needs and so makes itself more and more dependent on the material world.

I have not been able to reach this extreme degree of detachment. I have my little hut, which is simple enough, just one small room with a thatched roof, but it is solidly built of brick with a concrete floor. I have also a table, a chair, and a bed, which are luxuries for a sannyasi, but I have not been able to learn to sit and sleep always on the floor. I have also my books and my typewriter, but these are not really "mine," any more than the hut or the furniture — they are, as we say, "allowed for my use." A sannyasi is one who does not *possess* anything, not even the clothes on his back. He has renounced all "property." This is the real renunciation which is demanded, the renunciation of "I" and "mine." A sannyasi is one who is totally detached from the world and from himself. It is detachment which is the key word. It does not matter so much what material possessions you have, so long as you are not attached to them. You must be ready to give up everything, not only material attachments but also human attachments — father, mother, spouse, children — everything that you have. But the one thing which you have to abandon unconditionally is your "self." If you can give up your self, your "ego," you can have anything you like, spouse and family, houses and lands — but who is able to give up his or her self?[9]

"WHO AM I?"

I look at the flowers which are growing in the [ashram] garden outside my window — golden-orange marigolds and crimson Christmas roses. They come up out of the darkness of the earth, which is itself the shadow of the divine darkness, the abyss of being from which everything comes. They come out of this darkness into the light of the Word, radiant with its brightness, reflecting its glory. The impulse which quickens them in the earth and makes them thrust into the light is the movement of the Spirit, the divine *Shakti* [divine power], immanent in the earth. They come up into my consciousness, as the light touches the nerves of my eye and an image is formed in my mind. It is the same light of the Word which shines in them and in my consciousness. I see them in the light of the Word. And the same Spirit which stirs in them stirs in me, awakening feelings of joy and delight in their beauty. They are in me and I am in them, and both of us are in the Word and in the Spirit. This is a theophany. The Father speaks his Word and these flowers spring into being. He speaks again, and my consciousness awakens to delight in their beauty. He sends forth his Spirit and they are created. The same Spirit moves the flowers to spring and me to contemplate them: both in them and in me it is the one Lord who rejoices in his works.

Who am I? Let me try to answer this question. I am this person who sits here thinking and meditating. I am aware of myself sitting and thinking and meditating. I am aware of my body, which occupies the space of my cell, which looks out on the flowers in the garden and hears the birds singing, and at the same time I am aware of my mind, which reflects on my body and the world around me, which names these sights and sounds and expresses my thoughts in these words. But I am much more than this. I have a long history now of sixty-five years, in which my body and my mind have undergone innumerable changes.... I am formed of the matter of the universe and am linked through it to the remotest stars in time and space. My body has passed through all the stages of evolution through which matter has passed over millions of years....

How can I get to know myself? Not by thinking, for thinking only reflects my conscious being, but by meditating. Meditation goes beyond the conscious mind into the unconscious. In meditation I can become aware of the ground of my being in matter, in life, in human consciousness. I can experience my solidarity with the universe, with the remotest star in outer space and with the minutest particle in the atom. I can experience my solidarity with every living thing, with the earth, with these flowers and coconut trees, with the birds and squirrels, with every human being. I can get beyond all these outer forms of things in time and space and discover the Ground from which they all spring. I can know the Father, the Origin, the Source, beyond being and not-being, the One "without a second." I can know the birth of all things from the Ground, their coming into being in the Word. They come into being not in time and space, but eternally, beyond time, in the Word. The Word is the self-manifestation of the Father and the Self of all beings. I have existed eternally in this Word from the Father beyond time and space, and there we stand eternally before him.[10]

2

The Challenge of Hinduism

Time and again Bede Griffiths spoke of his coming to India as a search for "the other half of my soul." India was in the back of his thoughts from childhood — see the autobiographical excerpt that opens this chapter — but it came to the fore in the monastery. Monks connect instinctively with the common archetype that bonds them with Hindu sannyasis and Buddhist bhikkhus. *Father Bede's contemplative training at Prinknash predisposed him to take a further step in his ongoing monastic conversion by leaving Prinknash for India. The ecclesiastical canons to which he had submitted limited his freedom of movement, and it was necessary for him, first of all, to justify his departure by saying he was going to make a Benedictine foundation "in mission territory" and to petition the Holy See for a partial suspension of his vows (called an "indult of exclaustration"). He left England in 1955.*

Father Bede probably never saw himself as a "founder," but if he ever had such an illusion, it was soon dissipated by the realities he found on settling in Bangalore. His Indian Catholic traveling companion eventually changed his mind about founding a men's monastery and enrolled his own nieces in a new community of nuns. Father Bede did not remain long in Bangalore, because a Cistercian monk, who had arrived in India from Belgium two years after Bede, invited him to join in setting up a monastery for Syrian-rite Catholics in Kerala. Father Francis Mahieu was a man of strong personality, great intelligence, and boundless energy. He was the dominant figure at Kurisumala, while Father Bede became the gentle master of novices and guests.

A young Syrian-rite parish priest who came to join them in the early days has a vivid memory of Bede Griffiths. On the postulant's arrival he was told to present himself to the father master, who was working in the pineapple garden on the slopes below the monastery. The young priest found him there, pulling up the weeds, oblivious to the thorns that were scratching his already-bleeding arms. The following days the postulant observed him as, after the morning offices and the Qurbana, or eucharistic liturgy, he took an extremely frugal breakfast and went to the library, where he sat next to a window so that he could observe the arrival of any visitors and rise from his books to greet them. Father Bede's ascetical rigor was noted by all, monks or laypersons, who observed him in England and in India. It is paradoxical that he did not notice this quality in himself; writing to an American Dominican nun he stated, "We keep a more or less Cistercian observance [at Kurisumala], which I find rather hard, as I am used to an easier Benedictine way."*

Bede Griffiths was happy at Kurisumala, but he had not yet found the other half of his soul. Father Francis was primarily interested in interchurch ecumenism, while Bede wanted to have more direct contacts with Hindus. The opportunity for this came when, in 1968, Henri Le Saux (Swami Abhishiktananda) wrote Father Francis asking that he send two or three Indian brothers to take over Saccidananda Ashram at Shantivanam, as he, Abhishiktananda, had decided to reside at his other hermitage in the foothills of the Himalayas. Father Bede came instead (soon joined by two junior monks from Kerala).

Most people today speak of Shantivanam as "Bede Griffiths's ashram," but Father Bede himself reminded both his monastic

---

*From a manuscript letter, dated February 3, 1962, to Sister Janet Moore, O.P.

brothers and the guests that Monchanin and Le Saux were "our founders." He held them in profound veneration. Father Bede was supremely happy with his new abode — it represented everything he had been looking for in India. It seemed to him "my last resting place on my pilgrimage, and I can't expect anything beyond except heaven."*

Bede Griffiths wrote extensively on Hinduism, and commented on many of its sacred texts. On the whole his reading of India's greatest spiritual and mystical traditions was positive, and indeed, he regarded it as complementary to Western spirituality, dominated by the Jewish and Christian traditions. On a few points, however, he expressed reservations and even respectful criticism. His strongest demurral regarded the common notion of "reincarnation," which he found was spreading in the West, and he spoke of it with a certain irony: "Human persons get mixed up: you may have been Cleopatra in a past life, or somebody else. You are not yourself any longer, and in the end everything merges into one."† Insisting on the "complementarity" of Indian and biblical traditions, he affirmed the value of historical existence, central to the Bible's message. Historical time conveys the divine revelation of God's incarnation in Christ, a once-for-all event which nonetheless is of universal significance.

DISCOVERING INDIA

My first experience of India was when I was a small boy in the First World War. There was a convalescent camp for soldiers in the village where I was living, and one year it was occupied by Indian soldiers. I used to go and visit the soldiers, and one of them, a Sikh, became a good friend. He used to call me his "little brother," and when one of the soldiers offered me a

---

*Letter to Janet Moore, December 27, 1968.
† Bede Griffiths, *The Cosmic Revelation: The Hindu Way to God* (Springfield, Ill.: Templegate Publishers, 1983), 126.

cigarette (though I was much too young to smoke), he would point at me and say: "Sikh — no smoke" (the Sikhs as a rule neither drink nor smoke). I think I must have felt even then a kinship with India, and for a long time, when I was at school, it was my ambition to join the Indian Civil Service. Later, when under the influence of Tolstoy I became very strongly pacifist, I was attracted to Mahatma Gandhi. I remember reading a life of Lenin and Gandhi at this time and feeling how Lenin, with his belief in violence, materialism, and mass organization, stood for everything which I disliked, while Gandhi, with his faith in nonviolence and truth (*ahimsa* and *satya*), the spinning-wheel, and the village community, stood for all that I admired.

I had an opportunity of meeting Gandhi after this, and it is a lasting regret that I missed it. It was in 1931 when he came to London to the Round Table conference, and I was staying in Bethnal Green not far from where he was. I was undergoing a deep spiritual crisis at the time, which led to my becoming a monk soon after, and this prevented me from seeing him, but he and his conception of life remained fixed in my mind as an ideal which never left me. At the same time I became aware of the spiritual principles which underlay Gandhi's way of life by reading the Dhammapada and the Bhagavad Gita. This was my first introduction to Indian spirituality, and it left an indelible impression on my mind. The sense of an ultimate reality beyond this world of space and time, whether it was called Brahman or Atman or Nirvana, which alone gave meaning to life, became fixed in my mind, and I saw that the only way to reach this reality was by total detachment from the world. But I think that even then I was aware of what Gandhi saw so clearly, that this detachment was not a way of escape from the world but of a freedom from self-interest which enabled one to give oneself totally to God and to the world.

This was in accord with the lessons I had to learn gradually in the monastery during the following years. Christian asceticism, like Indian, is based on detachment, a radical separation from the world in order to give oneself totally to God. . . . But on the other hand, both in Indian and in Christian asceticism, one can see a corresponding movement of concern for the world, of the rediscovery of the world in God and of the service of one's fellow human beings out of love for God. This is evident in both the teaching and the example of the Buddha, but it was the Bhagavad Gita which gave this view its classic expression.

The great message of the Gita was that God can be found not only by the way of the ascetic in silence and solitude, but also by the householders in their daily duties, if they make the offering of everything they do to the Lord. It is this doctrine of selfless action, of working without seeking the "fruit of work," that is, of doing everything in a spirit of detachment from self and love for God, which inspired Mahatma Gandhi. . . . It is the same principle which has been at work in monastic life in the West, especially through the influence of the Rule of Saint Benedict. While the early Fathers of the Desert had been occupied, often exclusively, with the search for God alone, Saint Benedict, following on the example of Saint Basil, integrated the search for God with the life of the Church as a whole, that is, with the social order, and thus the monks of Saint Benedict came to lay the foundations of civilization in the West. The life of prayer was coordinated with both manual and intellectual work, and the monasteries became centers round which the economic and social life of the people was organized.[11]

COMING TO INDIA

My coming to India was due to my meeting with an Indian monk [Father Benedict Alapatt], whose lifelong desire it had been to introduce the monastic life into the Church in India. As there was then no monastery in India he had been professed as a monk in a European monastery, but was seeking for someone who would assist him in his enterprise. At first I saw no possibility of joining him, though I had already a deep love for India and a strong desire to go there. But in the course of time circumstances made it possible, and I received permission to accompany him to Bangalore to assist in a monastic foundation.[12]

When I first came out to India,...I thought that normal Benedictine life in the Latin rite, as it had come down in the Middle Ages in Europe, was all that was required. We began, in fact, a monastery of this kind near Bangalore soon after we arrived. We had a small bungalow in modern style outside a village [Kengeri], and we proceeded to furnish it in what I thought was the greatest simplicity, with just a few tables and chairs and beds and wash-stands. It was only after we had been living there for some time that I discovered that these were unheard of luxuries in most of the houses in the village, and only two or three of the richest people possessed them. In the same way, we wore our monastic habits with shoes and socks, but I realized after a time that these also were an expensive luxury.

It became clear, therefore, that if we wanted to approach the level of life not merely of the sannyasi, the monk, in India, but even of the ordinary villager, a drastic change would have to take place in our mode of life. But the experiment was valuable for many reasons. I was concerned above all to make contact with Hinduism, and Bangalore gave me many opportunities. In the village where we were living there were several university students, who soon began to come up to see us. When they found that we had many books on Indian life and philosophy, they were immediately interested and began to come up regularly. In this way many of them became our friends, and when I visited their houses I was able to see something of living Hinduism.... I also met several of the university professors and was able in this way to make contact with modern Hindu thought. In all alike, both students and professors, I found how deep was the influence of Hindu tradition on their life and thought, in spite of their modern education, and at the same time, how open they were to religious discussion.[13]

In the end it proved impossible to make a foundation in Bangalore, and [in 1958] we moved to Kerala at the extreme southwest tip of India. There we joined with Father Francis Mahieu, a Cistercian, who had come out to India with the same purpose, and eventually a monastery was established there.... It involved a new beginning in two important ways. In the first place, we adopted the Syrian instead of the Latin rite, as the majority of Christians in Kerala belong to the Syrian Church. This immediately opened up to us the whole world of Eastern Christianity, of which I had known little until then. Most people think of Christianity as an essentially Western religion, as it has largely become. But the Syrian Church is there to remind us that before the Church spoke Greek or Latin it spoke Aramaic, and while it was extending westward to Greece and Rome, it was also extending eastward through Palestine and Syria to Mesopotamia.[14]

Kurisumala Ashram...takes its name from Kurisumala, the "hill of the cross," a mountain among the high ranges of Kerala, below which the monastery lies. It is a beautiful position, looking over the hills to Anamudi, the highest peak in South India (nine thousand feet) on one side, and over the foothills and the plain to the sea on another. It is a wild and solitary place, not long ago the haunt of elephant and bison, but now joined to the plain by a new road which has been cut through the hills....

The monastery was given an ecumenical character from the beginning.... For this reason it was decided to adopt the *kavi* (saffron-colored) habit of the Indian sannyasi and to follow as far as possible the customs of a Hindu ashram. The tradition of *sannyasa,* or renunciation of the world, goes back to the earliest period of Indian history, and the *kavi* habit is common to both the Buddhist and the Hindu ascetic. It remains a living tradition in India today, and there are thousands of ashrams scattered all over the country. It was our desire to enter into this tradition of

Indian *sannyasa* and to establish a Christian ashram, in which
the life of prayer and asceticism could be followed along Christian lines, yet keeping always in touch with the traditions of
India.[15]

JULES MONCHANIN AND HENRI LE SAUX

The state of one who is engaged in the study of the Vedas is
brahmacharya, which can best be translated as "seeking God"
and which is held necessarily to involve the observance of
chastity. Moreover, those who have reached the final stage in
the search for God are called sannyasis, that is, [those] who
have made a total renunciation (*sannyasa*) of the world and live
in absolute poverty. It cannot be doubted that if the Church is
ever to penetrate deeply into the inner life of Hinduism, it will
be necessary to have Christian sannyasis who are prepared to
live in the same kind of poverty as the Hindu. . . .

The most serious attempt to follow this way of life in modern times is that of Father [Jules] Monchanin, a French priest
of saintly character and remarkable learning, who came out to
India [in 1939] to work under the bishop [of Tiruchirapalli,
Monsignor Mendonça] in the Tamil Nadu, not far from the
scene of [the seventeenth-century Jesuit sannyasi Roberto] de
Nobili's apostolate. After working for ten years as a poor parish priest in this district, he joined with a French Benedictine
monk, Father [Henri] Le Saux, to establish an ashram on the
banks of the sacred river Kaveri. . . . The ashram consisted of
small huts of brick with a concrete floor and a thatched roof
and no furniture, built in a mango grove by the banks of the
river. They had a small oratory built in Hindu style, the sanctuary taking the form of a *mulasthanam* (the inner shrine of a
Hindu temple), and a narthex for the people being attached in
the style of a *mandapam* (the outer court of a temple). Here
they lived in the utmost simplicity, wearing the *kavi* dress of the

Hindu sannyasi, going barefoot, sleeping on a mat on the floor, and adapting themselves in all their habits of food and behavior to Indian customs. Those who visited them there know how deep was the silence and solitude, the atmosphere of peace and of the "desert," in this ashram.

But there was more than this. Father Monchanin and Father Le Saux were both deep students of Hindu thought, but they also realized that the ultimate ground of meeting between the Church and Hinduism must take place not in the realm of thought but in that of contemplation. Behind all Hindu philosophy, behind all its search to know God, there is still a more profound impulse to experience the reality of God, to participate in the very being of God. This is the ultimate quest of the soul of India, which has inspired its religious tradition from the time of the Vedas to the present day. Unless the Church can answer this desire, unless it can show not merely that it possesses the true knowledge of God but also that it can lead souls to the experience of the truth, to that wisdom which passes all understanding, it will never reach the soul of India. This was an ideal for which Shantivanam (the "abode of peace") stood. It was to establish a school of the contemplative life in India which would correspond with the most profound aspirations of the Indian soul, to lead India to the fulfillment of its quest for the experience of God by showing that it could be found in Christ.

Unfortunately this initiative in the contemplative life met with practically no response. Indian Catholicism appears to be too deeply rooted in its fear of Hinduism (a fear based on ignorance) to be able to make this contact with the Hindu tradition at its deepest level. When Father Monchanin died rather suddenly in 1957, Father Le Saux was left alone, and externally nothing had been achieved. Yet it is difficult to believe that his work has failed. We must rather believe that he was a pioneer, the fruit of whose labors have yet to be seen. Like Charles de Foucauld, perhaps, he was ahead of his time, and we may hope that the seed which he planted will one day bear fruit.[16]

The whole life of Father Monchanin...centered on the Trinity. When he died in Paris in [October] 1957, he was meditating and discoursing on the Trinity on his deathbed. He was a great theologian; [he] said that *esse* (in Latin, "to be") is always *co-esse* ("to be with") — to be is to be in relationship. There is no such thing as being that is not in relationship. So the Being of Reality expresses itself in relationship, and the expression of this relationship is the Word of God. And then it communicates itself in love, in the Spirit, and the Spirit is the communication of being in love.

[The rational Greek mind] turned the Trinity into an abstract theological dogma which is totally unreal to most people. The reality is that Jesus communicates the Holy Spirit to us, and in the Holy Spirit he invites us to be one with the Father. It is part of our inner life. We are in the Holy Trinity. It is in us, and it is our life.[17]

LIFE IN THE ASHRAM

An ashram is not primarily a community like a monastery. It is a group of disciples gathered round a master, or guru, who come to share the prayer life, the experience of God, of the guru. The life, therefore, centers not on the common prayer of the liturgy but on the personal prayer of each member. It is the hour of meditation at dawn and at sunset, the traditional time for meditation in India, which forms the basis of the life, the silent communion with God, and the common prayer of the community is as it were an overflow from this.

In Shantivanam, the Forest of Peace, we each have a small thatched hut among the trees in which we live and pray, and we meet together for prayer three times a day, not for the formal prayer of the liturgy as at Kurisumala, but for a more informal prayer in which there are readings from the scriptures of different religions as well as psalms and readings from the Bible. In the morning we read from the Vedas, at midday from the Koran and the Granth Sahib of the Sikhs, and in the evening from the devotional poets, especially those of Tamil Nadu like the great Tamil mystic Manikka Vasagar. We are thus confronted day by day in our prayer with the question of the relationship between the different religions.[18]

In our ashram at Shantivanam we have a continual flow of visitors from all over the world, all in search of God, looking for a way of prayer and meditation that will enable them to discover their true selves, to integrate their personality, and to relate to the Church in a new and significant way. It is a bit saddening to see the number of people who simply leave the Church today because they cannot find the kind of prayer they are looking for. . . . Many Catholics come to the ashram who are no longer attending Mass, and after some weeks they spontaneously come back to Communion, to reading the Bible, to discovering the Church from *within.*

If you look at the Church from without, you can easily become alienated. When you learn to see what is behind the Mass, what is behind the Church, the Reality of Christ, then of course your whole life changes. That is what we have to help people to do, to see the inner mystery of the Church behind the outer forms. Many who have given up the practice of their faith seek a more authentic life. Some go to Buddhist monasteries, Hindu ashrams, to Sufis, but many, after some experience, recover their roots, as they say. . . . In their experience of prayer in our ashram, they often recover their faith and are able to see the Church in a new light, no longer from without but from within.[19]

WORSHIP AT SHANTIVANAM

The Vedas, which contain the germ of all the later developments of the Hindu genius, probably took their present shape in the second millennium before Christ, but their roots go back to far more ancient times and take us back to the very beginning of human speech. Perhaps nowhere else can one observe the process of human evolution from its primordial utterance to the most elaborate poetic speech and the most profound philosophy. The Vedas are known as *shruti,* that which has been "heard"; they are not merely the product of human ingenuity but of revelation, that is, an "unveiling" of the truth. They are also called *nitya,* that is, "eternal," signifying that they do not derive from this world of time and change but are reflections of the eternal. Finally, they are said to be *apaurusheya,* "without human authorship"; they are expressions of the eternal word, the *Vac,* and the human authors are *rishis,* "those who have seen" the truth, and "poets," *kavi,* those whose utterance is inspired. This shows how in ancient times speech — the word — was held to be something divine, a gift of God; and poets, those who had the gift of speech, were inspired by God.[20]

The typical rite of the Vedas was the fire sacrifice. I have seen several fire sacrifices, but they are rare and are performed only on great occasions. When the new temple was dedicated in our local village, seven altars were built and Brahmin priests were invited from various parts of the country to perform this sacred ritual, which took many days. . . . Today it is a rarity — the ordinary worship in the temple is called *puja.* A typical *puja* consists in offering the elements to God as a sign of the offering of the creation — earth, water, air, and fire. It can be performed in a big temple with many *pujaris* [officiants] and big crowds, or in a tiny village shrine among poor people, but it is always basically the same rite.

First of all they will put out come food on a plantain leaf, the fruits of the earth, rice with maybe a lemon, or some sugar cane. Then they will purify it with water. They make an offering of water, sprinkling it around the food which is to be offered to God, thus purifying it. Then they take incense, place it in a bowl, and wave it over the offering; this is called *arati* and signifies the offering of the air. Then camphor is burnt, which signifies the offering of fire. Camphor burns with a pure flame;

it burns itself out without leaving any residue. This is taken as a sign of the soul burning itself out in the service of God. This light is also waved around the offering. In this way the four elements are offered to God in the form of a cosmic sacrifice.

In the Mass of the Indian rite which we celebrate in our ashram we try to adapt ourselves to this form of sacrifice. At the offertory we first sprinkle water around the gifts and the altar. Then we sprinkle water on the people, and then the priest takes a sip of water to purify himself within. Thus we begin with the offering of water. Then we take the fruits of the earth, bread and wine,... and the work of human hands to the Divine. Then we take eight flowers and place them around the gifts in the eight directions of space, to signify that the sacrifice we offer is at the center of the universe. Every sacrifice in the ancient world was conceived as being offered at the center of the universe. They always related themselves to the whole cosmos. Then we take incense and wave it over the gifts, and in the same way we wave the fire, the flame of burning camphor over them.

The fourfold offering of the elements is to signify that the Mass is a cosmic sacrifice. Christ has assumed the whole creation. He is offering it in and through himself to his Father. He has not only taken us up into himself; he has taken up the whole of creation.

This is why the cosmic covenant has such importance for us. It enlarges our vision. We have become too human, too limited in our vision of life; we forget this great cosmic order through which God reveals himself all the time and which should be manifested in the Church. In this cosmic sacrifice, the whole creation is offered in and through Christ to the Father.[21]

WORD OUT OF SILENCE

From the earliest times...human beings have been aware of a mysterious presence, the sacred. All ancient religion had a profound sense of the sacred pervading the whole universe. In India it is still powerful in the villages, everywhere. It is basic to life. There is an awareness of a presence that awakens in you a word, a song, in response to the rhythm of nature. There is a great rhythm behind the whole universe, and when we chant or sing, we put ourselves in touch, in tune, with this rhythm. ...I was in a Benedictine monastery in England for twenty years. Chanting the Gregorian chant every day has a wonderful power; the ancient music puts you immediately in touch with the sacred....

Beyond music, there are certain words that open up the mystery of the divine presence. In India, the great word is *Brahman,* which comes from the root *brih,* meaning "to swell" or "to grow." Before there were temples, in the ancient Hindu tradition based on the *yajña,* the Vedic sacrifice, a fire was built in the courtyard of a house and offerings made. Agni, the god of fire in the heavens above, came down to the earth from the sun, consumed the offering, and brought it back to heaven. This was the way of relating the world to heaven. While the priest was offering the sacrifice, a word rose up within him, and he would say, "Brahman, Brahman," in response to the great mystery that was in the sacrifice....

Brahman, the Source of the universe, came to be used as the name for the Godhead as the power present in the sacrifice and in the whole universe. The word which came to be recognized as the supreme mantra, the word which for the Hindu, above all, invokes the presence of God, was the *pranava,* "OM" (which can also be spelled "Aum"). It is supposed to embrace all sounds. It has a tremendous sanctity in India. There is a beautiful text, in the Maitri Upanishad, which says, "There is an OM which is silent and an OM which is sound; and the sound comes out of the silence." Brahman was seen as the silence, and out of that silence comes this word, this OM, and then it returns to him. When we utter the OM, we are invoking the divine presence and surrendering ourselves to it. The OM takes us back to the Source, back to the Brahman.... A counterpart for Tibetan Buddhists is the phrase, OM *mani padme hum,* "OM, the jewel in the heart of the lotus." That is the jewel in the heart of the universe, the mystery in the heart of everything.[22]

BEING, CONSCIOUSNESS, BLISS

We are faced with the paradox that the ultimate truth, that which alone gives meaning to life, cannot be expressed, cannot in any ordinary sense be known. And yet it is above all to be known. "When this is known," as it is said elsewhere, "all is known." It is not known by sense or reason; it is known by an intuitive wisdom, which transcends our ordinary consciousness as much as rational knowledge transcends the knowledge of the senses. Yet if negation is the primary way of expressing this mystery, there is yet one affirmation which has always been considered to point to it more clearly than any other. This is the term *Saccidananda*. This term does not properly express or describe the mystery, but it signifies it more perfectly than any other words can do. The ultimate reality, the ultimate truth, is *sat,* "being," *cit,* "consciousness," and *ananda,* "bliss." This is as near as we can come to an affirmation of the nature of the Godhead. That the divine mystery is Being is clearly affirmed by the Katha Upanishad, where it is said: "Not by speech, not by mind, not by sight can he be apprehended. How can he be apprehended except by one who says, He is." But this "being" which is affirmed of the Godhead is not being in the ordinary sense; it is not the being of the logician or the philosopher. It is the transcendent mystery of being, beyond speech and thought.... It is this intuition of being, of the fundamental mystery of existence, which underlies all Hindu thought and finds expression in the Upanishads and the whole tradition of the Vedanta.

But this mystery of being is apprehended not merely as a concept, as in Greek thought, but as an experience. Being is experienced in consciousness of Being, not as the object but as the subject of thought. The being which is known is the Atman, the Self, the Person in its ultimate depth, and it is known not by an image or a concept but in an experience of identity.... In this reflection on itself, the mind discovers the infinity of Being in which it is grounded. It knows itself in the source of its being and of all being, in the source of all matter and life and consciousness. It discovers the identity of the Brahman and the Atman, the sources of being both of the universe and of the self, the ultimate truth, the ultimate reality. Such is the claim of the Upanishads and of all Hindu tradition. It is a claim which cannot be strictly verified, because this knowledge transcends all ordinary forms of consciousness and cannot therefore be properly expressed....

This brings us to the third aspect of this mystery, that of *Ananda,* or Bliss. This consciousness of being in nonduality is the source of endless bliss. It is beautifully compared in the Upanishads to the bliss of a man in the embrace of his wife: "As a man when embraced by a beloved wife knows nothing that is without, nothing that is within, thus this Person when embraced by the intelligent Self knows nothing that is without, nothing that is within." For this knowledge is not a bare, abstract knowledge of a merely rational consciousness; it is life and peace and joy. The soul enters into that depth of being, where all the powers of its being are gathered together. It is at the source of life, of the life of matter as well as of the mind; it is also at the source of love. For in this source of Being is the satisfaction of all desire. As it is said again in the Brihadaranyaka Upanishad: "Verily, not for the sake of the husband is the husband dear, but for the sake of the Self (the Atman, the Supreme Person). Verily, not for that sake of the wife is the wife dear, but for the sake of the Self," and so through all human relationships. It is this ultimate truth, this ultimate reality, which is the object of all human desire, without which no desire can ever be satisfied. We mistake the shadows of this passing world for the light which they reflect, and it is only when we discover the source of their being that our desire is satisfied.

This, then, is the mystery of being, of Truth, the Absolute, whatever we may like to call it, which is revealed in the Upanishads and to which all subsequent Hindu tradition bears witness. This experience has received different conceptual expressions, some of which may appear to be contradictory, yet in its full scope and depth it embraces all these conceptions. It is a mystical experience, transcending all concepts and capable of receiving different conceptual formulations.[23]

THE HINDU RENAISSANCE

There is no doubt that God has revealed himself in a wonderful way in India, for all these thousands of years. He has revealed himself in creation; he has revealed himself in the human heart; and above all, perhaps, he has revealed himself in a succession of saints.

Nothing moves the Hindu more than the attraction of these holy men [and women] who, from the time of the Vedas through the Buddha, from Rama and Krishna and the *bhaktas,* the "devotees" with their mystical poetry, to Shankara and Ramanuja, the great doctors of Vedanta, are a continuing source of inspiration right up to the present day. Hindus have their own particular saint whom they venerate as their guru and many others for whom they have a special devotion.…

This succession of saints represents a challenge to the Christian Church and to Western society. At present this challenge is only beginning to be realized. We are bound to face this challenge in all its dimensions, just as the Christian Fathers faced the challenge of Plato and Aristotle and Greek philosophy as a whole.[24]

From 1500 A.D. to the present day, there was a period of decline and renaissance. It is important to remember that the Hindu religion underwent a gradual decline, very like Christianity. Christianity in the eighteenth century was at a very low ebb; it was a period of universal skepticism. Hinduism suffered in a similar way. It seemed to be dying out, and all its worst abuses came to light. It was a period of universal decline. Hinduism has its dark side, as every religion has, and it reached its nadir in the eighteenth century. Then in the nineteenth century came the Hindu renaissance — and we have always to remember that we are now living in the middle of a Hindu renaissance.

It began with Ram Mohan Roy, a great Anglophile, who wanted to combine the wisdom of the Vedas with that of the Gospel. He was deeply impressed with the ethics of the Gospel and visualized a kind of synthesis, which led him to found the Brahmo Samaj [movement]. It was influential for a long time, and many people thought, at the beginning of the nineteenth century, that Hinduism would be converted to Christianity. English language and education [were] introduced at every level, and there was a strong missionary presence of various denominations. It appeared to be a great opportunity.

But God willed otherwise, and when Ramakrishna came, between 1836 and 1886, he renewed Hinduism in all its aspects. He was an almost illiterate Brahmin, yet a man of extraordinary holiness and extraordinary powers. He developed these powers from a very early age and became a great guru. [In 1901] his famous disciple Vivekananda organized an order in his name — the Ramakrishna Mission — which is still strong in the West as well as in India. He made of this neo-Hinduism a force in the world. From this beginning the renaissance has continued. That is why in India today conversion is extremely difficult, if not impossible. In all Christian colleges and schools, where there are hundreds of thousands of Hindu pupils, scarcely one becomes a Christian; and if anyone does, it arouses very strong feelings. Hindus are very sensitive about conversions. This is very important for our understanding of the situation in India. In their renaissance Hindus are recovering their ancient tradition — studying Sanskrit, reviving the Vedas, popularizing the Upanishads and the Bhagavad Gita, not to speak of Hindu music and dance. Yoga and Vedanta are being carried over to the West, especially to America, and there are schools of Yoga everywhere today. We are in the midst of that renaissance. This is the challenge to the Church today.[25]

HINDUS AND CHRISTIANS IN DIALOGUE

Hinduism is very much a living religion, and Hindus are keenly aware of its depth and antiquity; they call it the *sanatana dharma,* the "eternal religion." They say it has no beginning, that it goes back to the beginning of time, and they are making it known all over the world. That is why I feel that the Church today has been challenged. Christians are challenged to understand this religion, to enter into its inner depth, because it is essentially a mystical religion. It is not a matter merely of rituals and doctrines.... There is a common basis in the cosmic revelation, yet if one goes to a Hindu temple one may be completely mystified; it belongs to another world of symbols which are strange and bewildering.

Again if one starts with doctrines, the arguments are endless. There are innumerable Hindu doctrines which one can compare with similar Christian doctrines, but it is difficult to reach any agreement. But when one comes to the level of interior experience, that is where the meeting takes place. One of the two founders of our ashram in South India, Father [Henri] Le Saux,... wrote a book called *Hindu-Christian Meeting Point in the Cave of the Heart.* It is in this cave of the heart that the meeting has to take place.... We have to live this Hindu experience of God, and we must live it from the depth of our experience of God's revelation in Christ and in the Church. That is the challenge to us today.[26]

The question arises for the Christian: What is the point of preaching the Gospel? What have we got to say to the Hindu? This is made more difficult by the fact that Hindus are perfectly convinced that they have the whole truth.... Our founder, Father [Jules] Monchanin, came to India with a wonderful vision of an Indian Church, hoping for dialogue with Hindus. He was terribly frustrated because he found no curiosity among them. They feel they have the absolute and final truth....

All religions are, for them, included in this one truth. We have a neighbor in India, the head of an excellent ashram, a great pandit who goes around the country giving lectures and retreats. He has the absolute conviction that Vedanta [the chief Hindu philosophical system] is the one Supreme Truth and that all religions, including Christianity, are included in Vedanta. For them there is nothing to be learned. Christianity is simply one form of *sanatana dharma*...which developed in the West and is adapted to Western mentality. Islam is another form, which developed in the Middle East, in Arabia, and is adapted to those people. They always say that all persons can have their own religion; it can be any religion you like, but all religion is ultimately the same, and all end in the same identity of Being. For them there is no problem, there is no conflict, but there is also no dialogue.... In all my experience in India, in twenty-five years, I have hardly ever found an educated Hindu who is really open to dialogue, who really wanted to understand the Christian faith as something "other."[27]

[The dialogue with Hinduism] demands on our part an ever deeper understanding of the Hindu point of view and at the same time a clear grasp of the fundamental difference in the Christian point of view. The danger in the encounter with Hinduism is always that of a superficial syncretism, which would regard all religions as "essentially" the same, and only differing

in their "accidental" characteristics. Needless to say, this is de-
structive of all serious dialogue and makes real understanding
impossible.

What is required is a meeting of the different religious traditions at the deepest level of their experience of God. Hinduism
is based on a deep, mystical experience, and everywhere seeks
not simply to know "about" God but to "know God," that is,
to experience the reality of God in the depths of the soul. It
is at this level that Christian and Hindu have to meet, to discover, in their experience of God, what is really common and
where the real differences arise. It is here that we believe that a
monastery can play a decisive part. It should be the work of
[Christian monastics], by the practice of prayer and contemplation, to enter ever more deeply into the experience of God
and to seek for an even closer union with God in the depths
of the soul. Such an experience will lead [them] to understand
the Hindu mystical experience, as it were from within. But at
the same time, as [their] contemplation is centered on Christ,
it will lead not to that experience of "identity," which is the
tendency of all Hindu mysticism, but to the experience of "communion" with Christ, and through Christ with the persons of
the holy Trinity and with other persons in the mystical body of
Christ. . . . It is this witness to Christ, through a life lived in intimate union with him, which we believe to be the work of the
monk in India, and perhaps there is no more important work
in India today. Ultimately a Hindu will not be convinced by
arguments, but by a life lived in the closest intimacy with God.[28]

SOCIAL CONSEQUENCES
OF INDIAN PHILOSOPHY

I cannot help feeling that the present situation of India, with
its masses of poor, illiterate people, of people suffering from
disease and being left to die in the streets, really stems from

[India's] basic philosophy — all are caught in this wheel of *samsara* [the cycle of death and rebirth]. Your *karma* [the burden of your past deeds] has brought you to this state where you are dying in the street, but when you have died you will be reborn, and, please God, you will have a better birth next time. If one can help somebody else to have a better birth, if one can help others on their way, that is good; but there is no obligation to do it. *Karma* is working itself out.

This sense of cyclic time and constant recurrence can, of course, lead to a terrible fatalism, which can be sad but which can also be sustaining. The Hindu peasant, the poor person, has a wonderful capacity to endure, because he simply says, "All these things come from God" — disease, suffering, death, your child dies, your wife dies, all this is part of *karma,* part of the cosmic order....

The modern Hindu is trying to escape the negative aspect of myth, to realize more of the value of history, of matter, of science, and of progress. Dr. [Sarvepalli] Radhakrishnan, for instance, a leading scholar among Hindus, has been much influenced by the West and tries to bring out these aspects. But the opposite tendency remains very strong. That, I think, is the negative aspect of Hinduism.[29]

In no Hindu system does one find an adequate concept of creation. In the *advaita* ["nondualist"] doctrine of Shankara, the creation has no real being at all; it is an appearance of being with no more reality than the form of a snake which is mistakenly imposed on a rope. Brahman alone is being; the world is *maya* ["illusion"]. In the doctrine of Ramanuja, the world emanates from God as a "mode" of his being. It is the body of which he is the soul. The divine nature is "qualified" by the world. In the doctrine of Madhva, the world is indeed real and does not affect the nature of God; it is, moreover, totally dependent on God. But it exists eternally in this state of dependence on God; it is not given its existence by God. But this is the meaning of [the biblical doctrine of] creation. By creation the world has not only a real, though relative, existence dependent on God; it owes its existence to God. In Hinduism we have either to say that the world has no real existence in itself, or that it is an "appearance," a "manifestation" of God. This is not simply a matter of philosophical doctrine. It is rather a difference in the basic intuition of our relation to God. Israel learned from its experience of salvation an awareness of total dependence on God, and at the same time of [God's] absolute transcendence. This seems to have been a unique experience. Among no other people is there anything quite comparable to it, and the doctrine of creation derives from this unique experience.[30]

REINCARNATION AND RESURRECTION

In the Christian view, each individual person, body and soul, has a unique character, is a unique image of God, and that person will not dissolve. The more universal you become, the more deeply personal you become. You do not diffuse yourself, you do not lose yourself as you grow in knowledge and understanding and love — you extend. You do not cease to be a person. You become more deeply personal. Jesus is the most personal being in history, and yet he is the most universal....

It is true that Rama and Krishna also have a universal meaning, just as Buddha's Enlightenment has a meaning for all humanity. But the life and death and resurrection of Christ have not only a meaning for all, but also an effect on history.... The death and resurrection of Christ extends to all humanity, both in the past and in the present and in the future. In that sense it is a mythical event. It is a symbolic event, and yet it is also a historic event. Here history has assumed universal meaning.

The whole creation and the whole of humanity find an ultimate meaning, an ultimate purpose, in that death, resurrection, ascension, and final glorification.[31]

I am always hesitant about the idea of reincarnation as it is commonly understood, as the individual soul passing from one body into another. A deeper view of it may be [in the idea] that there is one Self which is manifested in all humanity. But while most of us are only aware of our own individual self with some little background beyond, those who have deeper knowledge are able to realize their relationship with the generations who have gone before....

The Buddha said he had experienced all his former births. It is a sign of intuitive wisdom to know not only one's isolated individual self, but oneself in the history of humanity. It may be compared with the words of Christ, "I say unto you, before Abraham was, I am" (John 8:38). Christ is the Word of God who unites all humanity in himself. This Word of God is manifested in the whole universe and in all humanity, and each of us participates in some measure in this one Word, the Self of all.... If we can know ourselves through and through, we can know humanity. The man of wisdom, the Buddha, the enlightened one, has the knowledge of humanity within himself. Christ, of course, is precisely man who "knew what is in man" (John 2:25). As the Word of God, he... knows all his past births, he knows all the past of humanity.[32]

It is not the individual soul that transmigrates; it is the Lord. The One Spirit is manifesting himself in all these individual consciousnesses.... The Lord who has taken a particular nature, and has lived his life in it, reassumes those elements into himself, and all that is left unfulfilled in that nature goes on to be manifested in another birth....

That makes sense from a Christian point of view. One can say that Christ is, as it were, incarnate in every human being; the whole of humanity is the body of Christ. That body is built up of all these cells of individual human beings. Sin enters into the body and disrupts it, and in the incarnation the Lord assumes the body of humanity, all these cells, all these individual lives into himself and restores them to their unity in the Self.

I think that this is worth reflecting on; otherwise from a Christian point of view transmigration is not meaningful. To say that individuals, when they die, are not going to meet Christ or to enter into eternal life, and that they are going to be reborn in this world, is contrary to the Christian view. But I think the [Bhagavad Gita] really supports the Christian understanding.... The Spirit, the Atman, enters into each individual and takes to himself the senses and the mind and enjoys himself in this world. But he is not affected by this experience, because he is completely detached. He experiences it, but it does not change his nature. So we each have in us an individual soul which is experiencing and which is suffering, and we also have the Eternal Spirit within us, presiding over us, working in us, and seeking to free us from our sin and from our limitation, and to bring us back to fulfillment.[33]

AVATARA AND INCARNATION

[The Bhagavad Gita] introduces the idea of the *avatara,* that is, the "descent" of God into the world. We should remember that there were ten *avataras,* or "incarnations" of Vishnu, and that Krishna [the chief protagonist of the Bhagavad Gita] was only one of them.... Vishnu appeared as a fish when the world was still under water. As the land was emerging from the waters, he came as a tortoise. When the land had fully appeared, he came as a boar. Then as animals developed into human beings, he came as a man-lion, half animal, half man. After that he came first as a dwarf, then as a full-grown man in the hero, the warrior Parashurâma. When humanity had reached the highest level of righteousness and wisdom, he appeared as Rama and Krishna. The Buddha was added [as an *avatara*] when Buddhism was absorbed into Hinduism. Finally came Kalki to bring the world process to an end. These are the ten *avataras* of the classical tradition, but some of the *Puranas* mention twenty or even forty. Hindus today tend to say that every age has its *avatara*....

There are obvious resemblances to the Christian idea of incarnation, and while we should not neglect what there is in common, we should also see what is different. First of all, the whole background of the concept of *avatara* is mythological. The fish and the tortoise, the boar and the man-lion are mythological figures. Even Rama and Krishna are only semihistorical. There may have been a historical Rama and Krishna, but they are more like Hector and Achilles or Agamemnon, the heroes of the Greek epics. Probably such beings existed, but many of the stories that have grown up around them are legendary. The same is true of Rama and Krishna; they have a mythological background. Secondly, the concept of the *avatara* belongs to cyclic time.... *Moksha* is liberation from this endless, cyclic existence, this wheel of time, this *samsara*. Being caught in the wheel of *samsara,* the good would always decline into evil, and the evil return again to the good. From this arose the concept of *moksha,* meaning liberation from the whole cycle of time, the final liberation. The theory of rebirth ["reincarnation"] also derives from cyclic time; one is born again and again in an endless cycle of births and deaths. The only way out is *moksha.*

Now the Hebrew-Christian revelation introduced a new understanding into this, namely, that time is in progress toward an end, an *eschaton....* The Bible is the record of God's revelation in history, and specifically in the history of Israel, beginning with Abraham, Isaac, and Jacob. The pattern was revealed in the deliverance from Egypt under Moses and the establishment of the kingdom under David. All this is God's revelation in the history of that particular people, and that history is gradually coming to a head, a fulfillment. In the New Testament— when time had been fulfilled, as the Gospel says — Jesus was born in historical time and [was] crucified under Pontius Pilate. Paul says, "It was his purpose in the fullness of time, to bring all things to a head in Christ." Monsignor [Ronald] Knox, in his translation of that verse, puts it very nicely, saying, "To give history its fulfillment, by bringing all things to a head in Christ."

The *avatara* is distinguished from the incarnation in belonging to cyclic time and to a mythological world and in manifesting itself again and again. With the *avatara* there is no fulfillment of history, no sense that this world of space and time is not simply to disappear but to come to its fulfillment. The Christian understanding is that God is working in history, and though there is a mythological background in the Old Testament, the story becomes more and more historical as time goes on. The books of Samuel and Kings, for instance, are historical books based on contemporary records, and when we come to the New Testament, everything centers on the historicity of Jesus, who was born under Augustus and crucified under Pontius Pilate. The incarnation in Christ is situated in history at a particular point of time, and in bringing everything to a head, it reveals the purpose of history. So the differences between incarnation and *avatara* are principally that the incarnation is historical, that it has finality, that it reveals the purpose of history and brings history to its fulfillment. That in turn makes a great difference in our understanding of human life.

In the Hindu tradition, the *avatara* is conceived as a play, a *lila* of God. All creation is a play, and human life is a play of God. Though there is something to be said for this view, it is obviously inadequate. When you think of all the terrible suffering in the world and the agonies which people endure, it is not enough to say that God is playing with them. The crucifixion is not a play at all; it is totally different. The idea of the New

Testament is that human history has a meaning and a purpose. We were born not merely to take part in a play, but each one of us has our own place in the plan of God, which is working toward a final culmination. Each life has a unique meaning. That purpose and meaning of history and of life are revealed in the historic person of Christ, in the historic events of his life and death and resurrection. That is the doctrine of incarnation.[34]

3

Awakening to the Feminine

*Women tended to frequent the ashram at Shantivanam in greater
numbers than men. Bede Griffiths always welcomed everyone as
persons, without making any distinctions. Women admired, even
loved him, because he was a man able to listen, to empathize, to
wait for them to express their questions before he volunteered
any answers. He was especially concerned with Indian Catholic
sisters, some of whom were seeking to lead a life more integrally
Indian, including the contemplative life of* sannyasa, *but they
were usually thwarted by their superiors and by the male clergy.*

*And yet you would not call Bede Griffiths a feminist. He sel-
dom dwelt on themes related to women's liberation, precisely
because his themes were universal and personal, equally appli-
cable to women and men. On one specific point his position
was clearly conservative and surprisingly in line with the traditional and current magisterium of the Roman Church. Once in
1992 Father Bede surprised a group of British listeners with the
statement: "Now, I think, we are beginning to see that we do
not need women priests. That would be putting the priesthood
back. We need a diversity of ministries where men and women
work together in the service of the kingdom of God. That, I
feel, is the model for the Church."* * After the talk, a questioner*

The Mystery Beyond: On Retreat with Bede Griffiths (London: Medio Media/
Arthur James, 1997), 76.

asked, *"Did I understand you to say that women do not have a valid vocation to the priesthood today?"* Bede replied, *"Oh dear no, I don't think women have a vocation to priesthood at all."**

The experience of his first stroke in 1990, about which you will read in the first excerpt of this chapter, raised Father Bede's consciousness of the feminine in general and of the feminine dimension of his own personality. Although he admitted to having repressed his sexual instincts as a young adult, his fondness then and later for the erotic themes in D. H. Lawrence's fiction and poetry betrayed his fascination with the male-female archetype.

Bede Griffiths's attitude toward sex was quite close to the paradoxical attitude of Indians, who on the one hand observe a sort of exterior "Puritanism" while on the other they deal with sex as a purely natural need, with few ethical implications. Father Bede's sexual ethics were quite traditional, although when counseling persons he used great pastoral tact and discretion, respecting always the individual's conscience.

Always a contemplative, Father Bede peered into the archetypal depths of the male-female dyad and saw there the key to the complementary relationship of peoples, cultures, and religions. Many regard the book Marriage of East and West *as his masterpiece; it was certainly his fullest statement on the relations between Christianity and Hinduism. Bede Griffiths was confident that the Church could find within itself the resources for a wide-ranging reform of its theology and ministry in the light of the new role of women in the family and in society. Hinduism's rich* shakta *tradition — the worship of the Divine Mother — can serve in part as a model and a stimulus for the rediscovery of the mother image of God according to the biblical and Syrian-Christian traditions. Likewise, Yoga as a practical art of meditation based on the body can aid Christians in*

----

*Ibid., 82.

overcoming the dualism which has resulted from Christianity's syncretistic contamination by Platonism.

Ultimately West and East must discover and fulfill each other in a sort of nuptial embrace which will enable human beings in the new global society to recover the inner and outer harmony which they have lost.

"SURRENDER TO THE MOTHER"

I will tell you of my experience when I had a stroke. It was in January 1990. I was meditating at six o'clock one morning, and something came and hit me on the head. It felt like a sledgehammer. Everything went blurred, like a television screen before it is focused. A terrible force was pushing me out of my chair, and I did not know what was happening. I managed to crawl on to the bed, and I was found there after about an hour. Apparently I was unconscious for a week. No, I was conscious, but I did not speak, and I have no memory of it at all. But there were some wonderful people in the ashram, and they arranged everything for me each day. At the end of a week I began to come round to normal consciousness, and there was a profound change.... I had died to the ego.... The ego-mind, and also...the discriminative mind that separates and divides, all seem to have gone. Everything was flowing into everything else, and I had a sense of unity behind it all. Then this began to open up. I thought I was going to die, and I...let go of the soul and body into the hands of God....

Then somebody came and massaged me, and I came back to normal. A very important experience then happened. I felt rather restless and uncertain, and an urge came to me to "surrender to the mother." I made this surrender, and an overwhelming experience of love came over me. It was like waves of love. I called out to someone who was watching there, "I am being overwhelmed by love!"

I think what happened was a psychological breakthrough to the feminine. In each person there is both masculine and feminine, and most men repress the feminine. I have done that to a very considerable extent, and I think it was the woman in me who came and hit me on the head! But then she came back to me as a loving mother. When you let the feminine open and your unconscious lets her come up, then she is the loving mother, and in coming back to you she transforms you. Because God is mother, we have to balance the masculine and the feminine in our nature. We must be aware of how we are repressing one aspect of our nature; by allowing it to come [forth] we become whole.

The stroke was a wonderful experience, and the greatest grace I have ever had in my life.[35]

MASCULINE AND FEMININE

"The woman gave me fruit of the tree, and I did eat," says the man in the story of Genesis. Who and what is this woman? Woman represents the intuitive power in human nature, while man represents the rational mind. These are two complementary aspects of human nature, and a human being is only complete when these two functions of human nature have been "married." It is important to recognize that these functions are complementary; both are equally necessary. Man and woman are equal and opposite. A woman does not become more equal to man by seeking to become like a man, but by revealing his opposite character. Yet it must be recognized that every man and woman is both male and female; reason and intuition exist alike in every human being, but in the man reason is dominant and intuition is subordinate.

In a perfect man or woman the "marriage" of opposites takes place, and in fact the very purpose of an exterior marriage is to enable the man and the woman to complete one another by an interior marriage. On the other hand, when reason and intuition, the man and woman, are separated, then disaster follows. Reason without intuition is intelligent but sterile; intuition without reason is fertile but blind. The woman who seduces man is the blind intuition which listens to the voice of the serpent, the animal intelligence, or sexuality. This is the normal course of sin. The feminine mind, instead of being guided by reason so as to open itself to the Spirit, and so to achieve the marriage of intuition and reason and the integration of the personality, surrenders to animal instinct and drags down the reason with it.

The serpent certainly has a sexual significance, but it is not that sex is evil. Sex is an animal instinct which, when the woman surrenders to the man and the man to the woman, becomes the means of their communion in the Spirit. Thus the serpent becomes the Savior, as it was said in Saint John's Gospel, "As Moses lifted up the serpent in the wilderness, so must the Son of Man be lifted up, that whoever believes in him may have eternal life." It is the separation of sex from intuition or feeling and from reason and understanding which is the cause of sin, while the integration of the sexual instinct with feeling and imagination — that is, the intuitive mind — and with reason and will — that is, the rational mind — brings about fulfillment of both man and woman in the life of the Spirit.[36]

In the West today the masculine aspect, the rational, active, aggressive power of the mind, is dominant, while in the East the feminine aspect, the intuitive, passive, sympathetic power of the mind, is dominant. The future of the world depends on the "marriage" of these two minds, the conscious and the unconscious, the rational and the intuitive, the active and the passive. In India and all over the world today these two minds are meeting, but often the impact of the West on the East is that of a violent aggression, whether by armed power, as in the past, or by the much more subtle aggression of science and technology. . . .

Yet it still remains possible to conceive of a development of science and technology which would not seek to dominate nature in the style of the West but to work with nature, building up from the basis of the village economy, as Mahatma Gandhi sought to do, and so create a new culture, in which humankind and nature, reason and intuition, the Yang and the Yin in Chinese terms, would be brought into harmony.[37]

GOD AS MOTHER

The Father-God is a serious problem for many people, especially for those who have a psychological history with their own father to work through.... In India the mother image has always been stronger than the father image. Indians use both and will quite spontaneously speak of God as "my mother, my father." So strong is their sense of the motherhood of God that if you want to find the Catholic church in an Indian village you ask for the *matha kovil,* the mother-church where our Lady is. Our Lady has a tremendous power, and for most Catholics it is the only archetype of the feminine. But this motherhood should be in our idea of God. God is no less mother than father, and so we are trying to develop a theology in which we can see the Holy Spirit as mother.

In Hebrew, the word *ruah,* "spirit," is feminine;... *hokmah,* the wisdom of God, is always feminine too. In the book of Proverbs, she played before God at the creation of the world.... Originally even the "word of God" was feminine, as in Sanskrit. So we have to get used to thinking of God as both masculine and feminine; the one is needed to balance the other. It is urgent for most people to move beyond the exclusively masculine image, and this is an important part of theological development today.[38]

The mystery of the Godhead, of ultimate Truth and Reality, is to be found not in a personal God nor in an impersonal

Absolute but in interpersonal relationship, or a communion of love. The universe has been called a "complicated web of interdependent relationships" ([Fritjof] Capra), and humanity as a whole can be described as a web of interpersonal relationships. Every being seeks spontaneously to express and communicate itself, and the whole universe can be conceived as a mode of expression and communication in space and time of the one, infinite, and eternal Reality. In a human being this expression and communication comes through consciousness which manifests itself as knowledge and love. The supreme Being or absolute Reality therefore comes to be conceived as expressing itself in an eternal Word or Wisdom, which is manifested in the structure of the universe and in the human heart, and communicating itself in a Holy Spirit or divine Energy, which is manifested in all the energies of the universe and in human beings above all in the energy of love. It is in this way that the Godhead comes to be conceived as a Trinity. The Father, the Ground and Source of being, expresses himself eternally in the Son, the Word or Wisdom which reveals the Godhead, and the Holy Spirit is the Energy of Love, the feminine aspect of God, by which the Godhead eternally communicates itself in Love. All human wisdom and love is a manifestation in space and time of this eternal Wisdom and Love. In Christian tradition the Word of God is conceived to have received its full and final revelation in Jesus Christ, and the Spirit of God to have been revealed in the fullness of love manifested in his sacrifice on the Cross and present in the Church as the Spirit of love, communicated to every Christian.

It is here that the feminine aspect of God is revealed, though it has rarely been recognized in the Christian tradition. If the Son is "begotten" of the Father, there must clearly be a Mother in whom he is conceived. In the incarnation the Son was conceived in the womb of the Virgin overshadowed by the Holy Spirit. In eternity the Son is begotten of the Father and conceived in the womb of the Mother, the Holy Spirit, just as in creation the Father sows the seed of the Word in matter, and the Holy Spirit, the Mother, nourishes the seed and brings forth all the forms of creation. In the Hindu tradition the world comes forth from the union of Purusha and Prakriti, the Male and Female principles, and in Sufi doctrine the world is brought into being by the "Breath of the Merciful...." In Hindu and Buddhist tradition sexual love has always been seen as a symbol of divine love. Ibn al Arabi's expression "Breath of the Merciful" (*nafas al rahman*) is especially significant, since the word *rahman* comes from the root *rahima,* which means "womb." The "merciful" is thus conceived as the womb from which all the potentialities in the divine mind are released in creation.[39]

THE FEMININE IN CHRISTIANITY AND HINDUISM

It is in the Holy Spirit that the feminine aspect of the Godhead can be most clearly seen. She is the *Shakti,* the power, immanent in all creation, the *receptive* power of the Godhead. The world comes forth from the Father, the eternal Ground of Being, in his Word, the Cosmic Person (Purusha). In him the ideas and archetypes of all created beings are hidden; he is the exemplar of all creation. But it is the Spirit who conceives these "ideas" in her maternal womb and brings them forth in creation. She is the Great Mother (the *Devi*), who nourishes the seeds of all beings and makes them grow. Still more, she is the mothering Spirit in humankind, who receives the Word, the Wisdom of God, in her heart, of whom in the Christian tradition Mary is the figure, receiving the Word of God in her heart and bringing him forth in his earthly manifestation. Even in the bosom of the Godhead itself, the Spirit is the eternal feminine, who on the one hand receives the Word of God coming from the Father, and on the other is the Bride of the Son, through whom the creation is conceived and brought into being....

In Christian tradition the figure of the Mother is found [also] in the Church. In an early Christian writing, *The Shepherd of Hermas,* the Church appears in the form of an old woman. When it is asked why she appears as an old woman, the answer is given: "Because she was created first of all. On this account she is old, and for her sake the world was made." It is necessary to see the Church in this cosmic aspect. The Church as a historical institution has a very recent origin and occupies a very small part of the world. But the Church in herself is the eternal Mother; she is the created aspect of the uncreated Spirit. "For her sake the world was made." The world in a real sense is the "becoming" of God. He, who is infinite, unchanging being in himself, reveals himself, expresses himself, in the finite, changing nature of the world. The eternal Word, in whom the "archetypes" of all created beings exist eternally, manifests himself in time. The whole creation, from the smallest atom to the furthest star, is a manifestation in space and time, in multiplicity and change, of that unchanging One. The Spirit, immanent in nature from the beginning, receives these "seeds of the word" into her womb and brings them forth in creation. From the first beginning of matter, through all the stages of evolution, of organic growth and consciousness, the Spirit is structuring these forms, molding them by her inherent power.

In us this Spirit is at work organizing the chemicals which make up our body, building up the cells, developing the nerves and the muscles and the glands, structuring the organs of touch and taste, of smell and sight and hearing, finally bringing all this complex organism, through the elaborate structures of the brain, into consciousness. With consciousness, Nature, the Mother, awakens to a new mode of being, and begins to discover, to become conscious of, her meaning and destiny. Over millions of years the Spirit is working through Nature, responding to the action of the Word, the Cosmic Person, the Purusha, who unites himself with his bride, his *Shakti,* to bring forth this world. As consciousness grows in humankind, Nature becomes conscious of the immanent power within her, and the Church is born....

It is not only the whole of humanity but the whole creation which constitutes the body of the Church. Matter was created from the beginning with an innate tendency toward life and consciousness. Human consciousness was created from the beginning with an innate tendency toward the final and perfect consciousness of the Spirit. The same Spirit was present in matter, in life, and in human beings, from the beginning drawing them toward itself. In Jesus this movement of matter and consciousness toward the life of the Spirit reached culmination. In him the divine consciousness took possession of human consciousness, and both body and soul, matter and consciousness, were transformed. In him the marriage of God and humankind, of nature and Spirit, of Purusha and Prakriti, was consummated.[40]

HUMANKIND AND NATURE
SEPARATED AND REUNITED

All of us once upon a time, when we were in the womb, were in perfect harmony with nature; we were part of the great Mother herself. Every human being [unconsciously remembers] this original oneness, this total harmony. The child too, after it is born, if it is loved and cherished, may experience something of this original wholeness. Many primitive people also, like the Pygmies in central Africa, who live very close to nature, feel themselves to be one with nature. They have an intuitive awareness of their bonds with the plants and animals and live in the cosmic harmony of day and night, summer and winter, birth and marriage and death.

But as reason develops, and they eat of the tree of knowledge, a division grows between human beings and nature. Human beings feel themselves separate from nature; the world becomes their enemy; violence and conflict take the place of the original peace. But there is no going back to Eden; they cannot return to that state of innocence when their consciousness was not divided. They have to advance through trial and conflict to a communion with nature at a deeper level of consciousness. The danger is that as the rational mind develops and human beings become capable of controlling the forces of nature, they seek to dominate nature and use it for their own purposes. This has been the course of history in Western Europe and America and has led to the present state of conflict, where human existence is threatened by the forces which have been released.

But there is another way, by which, as reason develops and a scientific knowledge gives man the capacity to control the forces of nature, he enters into a new relationship. The rational mind enters into communion with the intuitive mind, and humankind and nature are "married." The male ceases to dominate the female or to be seduced by her, and a marriage of equals takes place. Both the man and the woman are made whole by marriage. The objective world is no longer an enemy to be subdued but a partner in marriage. There is a saying in one of the apocryphal Gospels: "When will the kingdom of God come?" And the answer is given: "When the two shall be one, when that which is without is as that which is within, and the male and the female shall be one." This is the return to Paradise, the reversal of the effects of the Fall.

In Paradise, human beings had been in harmony with nature, with themselves, and with God. Sin had brought division between human beings and nature, between man and woman, and between human beings and God. In the plan of redemption this threefold harmony is to be restored. Therefore the promise is made to Abraham of a land where he shall dwell securely, signifying the reconciliation of human beings and nature. Then he shall become a great people in which all races of the world will be blessed, signifying the restoration of humankind to its original wholeness. Finally, God will come to dwell in this people: "You shall be my people, and I will be your God."

The symbolism of the land is brought out most clearly in the Letter to the Hebrews. This letter...was probably written in Alexandria, where the tradition of Platonism, with its deep sense of symbolism, was preserved. Thus it is said that the gifts and sacrifices offered in the temple were only a copy and a shadow of the heavenly sanctuary. All earthly rites and ceremonies are in Plato's sense "copies" of eternal realities. So it was that the promised land came to be seen in a new light. When Abraham went out, it is said, to go to a place which he was to receive as an inheritance, he did not know where he was to go. He was journeying in search of an unknown country, seeking a homeland. The land which he was seeking was not that from which he came out; it was a "better country, that is, a heavenly one." Here we can see the passage from the literal to the symbolic sense, from a this-worldly religion to an other-worldly religion.

Our desire for a homeland can never be satisfied with anything in this world. The passionate desire of so many people to find a homeland is a sign of this desire for something beyond this world. Yet there is a deep sense in which this desire is genuine. We do not desire a state in which there will be no earth, no bodily nature. We desire the satisfaction of our bodily desires, a communion with nature in which the profound awareness of our oneness with nature will be realized, a communion with one another in which the deepest intimacy of sexual union will be experienced. This was marvelously expressed by the prophet Isaiah when he said, "You shall no longer be termed Forsaken, and your land Desolate, but you shall be called My-delight-is-in-her, and your land Married; for the Lord delights in you, and your land shall be married. For as a young man marries a virgin, so shall your Rebuilder marry you, and as the bridegroom rejoices over the bride, so shall your God rejoice over you."

All this takes place only in the new creation, when soul and body are transfigured by the indwelling Spirit, when the "land" is no longer seen as an exterior object but is experienced within as the soul's eternal ground, and the man and the woman are united not in an external marriage but in the interior marriage which takes place in God, that is, in the inner depth of the Spirit, beyond time and space.[41]

YOGA, THE WAY OF UNION

Each chapter of the Bhagavad Gita concerns a particular Yoga. [The] first chapter is called "The Yoga of Arjuna's Despair," and it is significant that the experience of despair is a Yoga; despair is often the first step on the path of spiritual life. It is very important to go through the experience of emptiness, of disillusion, and despair. Many people do not awaken to the reality of God and to the experience of transformation in their lives until they reach the point of despair.

The term "Yoga" is one of the basic words in the Gita. It has many meanings, but the root of the word is the same as the Latin *jugum* and the English "yoke." The normal meaning is "union" or "integration," which refers to the goal, but it is important to realize that the steps by which we approach union are also Yoga. The union is primarily union with God, but it involves the uniting or integrating of all aspects of our being.[42]

The transformation of body and soul by the Spirit is the work of Yoga. In the classical system of Patañjali [author of the *Yoga Sutras*] there are two principles which govern not only human life but the whole creation. One is the masculine principle, Purusha, who is pure consciousness; the other is the feminine principle, Prakriti, who is the source of all the activity of nature. The cause of all suffering in this world is that Purusha, consciousness, has become entangled with Prakriti and becomes subject to the passions of nature. The art of Yoga is to separate

Purusha from Prakriti, consciousness from the actions and passions of nature, so that consciousness becomes free from every movement of nature and enjoys the bliss of pure contemplation, untouched by any taint of mortality.

This ideal of *kaivalya,* of total separation from the world, has been present in Hinduism from early times, and for Shankara [eighth century C.E.] this remains the goal of life. All the activity of nature is *maya:* it is an illusion due to ignorance. Wisdom consists of the knowledge of being in pure consciousness without any modification, and this brings lasting bliss — *Saccidananda* — the bliss of the pure consciousness of being. There is certainly a profound truth in this doctrine. There is an experience of being in pure consciousness which gives lasting peace to the soul. It is an experience of the Ground or Depth of Being in the center of the soul, an awareness of the mystery of being beyond sense and thought, which gives a sense of fulfillment, of finality, of absolute truth. And indeed there is a sense in which this experience is ultimate. It is an experience of the undifferentiated Ground of Being, the Abyss of Being beyond thought, the One without a second. But does this mean that all other modes of consciousness are illusory, that nature has no reality, that the experience of God is also an illusion?

Though Shankara has many followers among Hindus today, his doctrine has never gained universal acceptance. It has been opposed from the beginning by the Vaishnava philosophers, who were devoted to a personal God: Ramanuja, Madhva, Nimbarka, Vallabha, and Chaitanya [from the eleventh to the sixteenth centuries], who have constructed rival systems of Vedanta in opposition to Shankara — and it is rejected by Shaiva Siddhanta [the principal current of South Indian philosophy and mysticism]. Moreover, in modern times it has met with opposition from those philosophers who, under the influence of the West, have recognized the values of matter and life, of history and personality, of whom Sri Aurobindo [d. 1950] is the greatest. In his philosophy there is a wonderful synthesis, based on the Vedanta, of ancient and modern thought. In him the values of being and becoming, of spirit and matter, of the One and the many, of the eternal and the temporal, of the universal and the individual, of the personal God and the absolute Godhead, are integrated in a vision of the whole, which has never been surpassed in depth and comprehensiveness. In the integral Yoga of Sri Aurobindo, the values of matter and life and human consciousness, and the experience of the personal God, are not lost in the ultimate Reality, the divine Saccidananda. Matter and life and human consciousness... are seen to be evolving toward the divine life and the divine consciousness, in which they are not annihilated but fulfilled.

This is the goal of a Christian Yoga. Body and soul are to be transfigured by the divine life and to participate in the divine consciousness. There is a descent of the Spirit into matter and a corresponding ascent, by which matter is transformed by the indwelling power of the Spirit, and the body is transfigured....

For the Christian, this has already taken place in the resurrection of Christ. In his body, matter has already been transformed so as to become a spiritual body which is the medium of the divine life. The human body, by contact with this body of Christ, which is no longer limited by space and time, has within it the seed of the divine life. As Saint Paul says: "We ourselves, who have the first fruits of the Spirit, groan inwardly as we wait for...the redemption of our bodies." And this "groaning" is part of the travail of all nature, which waits to be delivered "from its bondage to decay and obtain the glorious liberty of the children of God." This is the cosmic drama, this transformation of nature, of matter and the body, so as to become the outward form of the divine Spirit, the body of the Lord. And this transformation is taking place in our own bodies. In every human being, matter is being transformed daily into Spirit. We take in matter through our bodies as food, and that matter goes to feed the brain, and the brain produces thought. Thought itself is matter become Spirit. But for most of us this process remains incomplete. Matter is never fully assimilated by the Spirit, and at death the matter unassimilated by the Spirit returns to the earth. But in the body of Christ we can see that transformation of matter by Spirit taking place, which is the destiny of us all at the end of time. The body of the Virgin Mary is said to have been transformed in the same way, and doubtless there are other saints and yogis of whom this is true.[43]

In Indian thought, as Sri Aurobindo remarked, there has been a "revolt of spirit against matter," and the tendency has been to see human destiny in terms of a "release" from material being. In the ultimate state, according to Shankara, there is no place for matter; there is nothing but pure consciousness, which is the state of pure spirit. In the philosophy of Ramanuja also, the soul is essentially a spiritual being which finds its happiness in the contemplation of God. The body is like a suit of clothes or, as he says, like dust on a diamond, which hides the pure spirituality of the soul and has eventually to be shed. But in the Christian view, the soul and body together make up the human person. The soul grows into consciousness through the body, experiences itself through the body, and seeks always to penetrate the body with its consciousness. The aim of evolution is, therefore, not to separate soul and body, but to render the body — and hence matter as a whole — more and more open to the influence of the soul, that is, of consciousness, so that eventually the body is transfigured and becomes the pure expression of the spirit. It is the great merit, among Indian thinkers, of Sri Aurobindo to have realized the full significance of matter in the ascent of evolution and to have given it its proper place in the plan of creation.[44]

THE MARRIAGE OF EAST AND WEST

I come back again to ask, as I have done many times before, "What has India taught me, and what has she to teach the world?" It seems to me as to many others today that we are entering on a new age. The age of Western domination is over, and the future of the world lies not in Western Europe and North America but in Asia, Africa, and Latin America. This does not mean that we have to reject the Western heritage. The ideas of Western science and democracy have penetrated to every part of the world. The ideal of Western science, of the accurate observation of phenomena, of rational analysis, free from all partiality or emotional bias, of the discovery of the "laws" of nature, that is, regular patterns of events, and of their application for the benefit of humankind — these ideas remain of permanent value. So also the principles of democracy, of the value of the individual person, of the "rights of man," that is, the right of the individual to life and growth and health and education, above all, the right of self-government in whatever political structure it may be expressed, and, it need hardly be said, the right of woman to equality with man — these are marks of the growth of humanity to greater maturity, to a greater realization of what it means to be human.

But the limitations of Western science and democracy have become more and more evident. The disastrous effects of Western industrialism, physical, social, and psychological, polluting the world and threatening to destroy it, are only too evident. But this is not an "accident" due to the misuse of science and technology; it is due to a fundamental defect in Western man. By "Western man" I mean, of course, not simply men and women who live in Western Europe and North America, but the peculiar culture which derives originally from Socrates and the Greek philosophers and has in the course of time produced the typical Western man who is to be found all over the world today. Western science and democracy are an inheritance from the Greeks. For a long time, from the time of Christ until the Renaissance, this Greek culture under the direction of Rome permeated both Eastern and Western Europe and built up a unique culture, in which the genius of Greece and Rome blended with the oriental Semitic culture of the Christian religion to create a balanced and harmonious way of life, which has left its record in the architecture, the art, the poetry, the philosophy and theology of the Middle Ages. But at the Renaissance this harmony was lost, and the dominant, aggressive, masculine, rationalist mind of the West took charge, so that Europe remains today in a permanent state of imbalance.

The balance can be restored only when a meeting takes place between East and West. This meeting must take place at the deepest level of the human consciousness. It is an encounter ultimately between the two fundamental dimensions of human nature: the male and the female — the masculine, rational, active, dominating power of the mind, and the feminine, intuitive, passive, and receptive power. Of course, these two dimensions exist in every human being and in every people and race. But for the past two thousand years, coming to a climax in the present century, the masculine, rational mind has gradually come to dominate Western Europe and has now spread its influence all over the world.

The Western world — and with it the rest of the world which has succumbed to its influence — has now to rediscover the power of the feminine, intuitive mind, which has largely shaped the cultures of Asia and Africa and of tribal people everywhere. This is a problem not only of the world as a whole, but also of religion. The Christian Churches, Catholic, Orthodox, and Protestant, have all been shaped by the Western mind. They have built up structures of doctrine and discipline, of law and morality, which all bear the impress of the Western genius. The Eastern Churches have retained something of an Oriental character but are still dominated by the Greek mind. Even the original Semitic tradition, which gave birth to Christianity, though deeply intuitive has still a dominantly masculine character. All the Christian Churches, Eastern and Western, have to

turn to the religions of the East, to Hinduism, Buddhism, Taoism, and the subtle blend of all these in Oriental culture, and to
the deep intuitions of tribal religion in Africa and elsewhere,
if they are to recover their balance and evolve an authentic
form of religion which will answer to the needs of the modern
world.[45]

4

A New Age

During the summer of 1984, while I was at Shantivanam, the reading during meals — always carefully chosen by Father Bede — was from The Aquarian Conspiracy *by Marilyn Ferguson. The book reviewed the multitude of unconnected movements and tendencies which were just beginning to be labeled "New Age" by the secular press. The book was also being read with attention and alarm in the Vatican, and in some ecclesiastical circles it aroused a state of panic akin to the American "red scare" of the 1950s. On the contrary, what should be evident to any intelligent reader is the extreme weakness and ephemeral character of many of these phenomena, although the profound spiritual malaise of contemporary people, of which the so-called "New Age movement" is a symptom, is to be taken seriously.*

Bede Griffiths always had an attitude of deep reverence before the mystery of every human conscience, and he treated with the utmost respect each individual's search for meaning and for spiritual unfolding. He realized time and again that the religious formation many people from the West had received had stunted their inner growth and had provoked one of two possible reactions: either the rejection of every form of institutional religion or the trek toward India and beyond in search of a spiritual guide. Many of these alienated Westerners found this guide in Bede himself.

From the balanced and discreetly critical way he spoke of Hinduism — especially of some of its tenets, like karma *and* "reincarnation" *— it should be evident that Bede Griffiths cannot be lumped together with the crowd of teachers and channelers who populate the New Age planet. Yet his mind and heart instinctively moved in liberal channels. He welcomed the changes in the Catholic Church after the Second Vatican Council, while remaining deeply traditional in the grounding of both his religious understanding and his ethical and ascetical practice.*

In a way, a Benedictine monk can afford to be a traditionalist, because the monastic tradition is itself a "liberal" current in the Church, at least in its first phase in history, from the fourth century to the eleventh. Bede, formed in the cenobitic rigor of the congregation of Subiaco, felt instinctively akin to Saint Romuald of Ravenna (ca. 952–1027), father of the "rational hermits," the Camaldolese Benedictines. Like Romuald, Bede lived his monastic stability in a paradoxically mobile observance; both were called hermits, and yet neither was jealous of his privacy. What the monastic heritage gave to Bede Griffiths was a concrete, historically realized model of an alternative society. He did not propose maintaining its fixed, institutional models of rigid cloister and same-sex communities, and he was delighted to discover in the micro-history of the Camaldolese the simple, eremitical coenobium and the joint communities of nuns and monks.

Another kindred soul Griffiths found in Mahatma Gandhi, for whom he had a profound veneration. In both we see the fusion of a strong grounding in traditional values, ethical and religious, with a breadth of mind that enabled the one to break with certain deeply rooted taboos and prejudices of Hindu tradition and the other to recognize in the Gandhian ideal an authentic expression of the ethical heart of Christianity.

From his youth Bede Griffiths was a strong critic of industrial, technocratic society; he placed no hopes in its transformation from within, and he expected the negative forces it had set

*in motion to bring its own downfall. In the final years of his life,
Father Bede connected with the "green" and environmentalist
movements; although he seriously entertained the possibility of
a catastrophic breakdown of the planetary ecosystem, he preserved the heartfelt hope that from its ashes a new world order
would arise.*

A CHANGING CHURCH

When I wrote *The Golden String,* telling the story of my search
for God which led me to the Catholic Church and to a Benedictine monastery, I thought that I had reached the end of my
journey, at least as far as this world was concerned. But in fact,
even while I was writing *The Golden String,* a new era was
about to begin in my life, which was to bring about changes
as profound as any that had gone before. I had been led to the
discovery first of God, then of Christ, and finally of the Church.
But now I had been led in a strange way to retrace the path
I had taken and to make new discoveries about God, about
Christ, and about the Catholic Church. It was as though I had
been climbing a mountain and, having reached the peak, discovered further ranges beyond with new peaks, opening up a
new horizon.[46]

[In the 1950s] the boundaries both of the Church and of
the monastic life and their relation to the world seemed to be
fairly fixed, but since the Second Vatican Council the whole
perspective has changed.... These changes had been prepared
in my case by the biblical, the liturgical, and the ecumenical
movements, which had shaped my thought when I was writing
The Golden String. But Vatican II has carried these movements
further than I would ever have expected. Biblical criticism,
Catholic and Protestant alike, has advanced to a point where
we have to see the whole biblical revelation in a new light. The

liturgical movement, by the introduction of the vernacular instead of the traditional Latin, has opened the Roman Church to
other cultural traditions in a way which must gradually change
the very structure of the Church. The ecumenical movement, by
opening to other religions, has brought the Church into contact with other religious traditions in a way which is producing
radical change in the relation of Christianity to other religions.

The most radical change which has taken place has been in
the understanding of the temporal and historical character of
the Bible and the Church. The Bible, instead of being regarded
as a fixed and final revelation..., is seen as a historic process
in which the Word of God is being revealed under changing historical conditions, shaped by the historical, psychological, and
cultural circumstances of a particular people, and Jesus himself has to be seen as the Word of God "made flesh" under the
conditions of a particular historical situation. In the same way
the dogmas of the Christian faith can no longer be regarded as
fixed and final statements of Christian faith, but as expressions
of Christian faith, guided by the Holy Spirit, but always con-
ditioned by particular historical circumstances and capable of
ever new expression.[47]

SEARCHING FOR
AN ALTERNATIVE SOCIETY

When [in 1930, after our graduation from Oxford,] I and my
friends were led to reject the industrial revolution and to try to
shape our lives by a simpler and more traditional way of life, we
were almost blindly seeking an escape from the world in which
we had grown up and trying to discover a more natural way of
life on our own. But since that time this rejection of the present
system of civilization has spread throughout the world. Everywhere there is a search for an "alternative society," a way of

life which will be more natural and more human and is equally opposed to the capitalist and the communist systems.

I myself was led to the discovery of religion and Christianity as giving a meaning to life, and to the monastic life as an alternative way of life. Yet it is clear that religion and Christianity, and to a large extent monasticism, are caught up in the present system and have failed to offer the way of life which people are seeking.

It would seem that we have come very near to the state of the Roman Empire in the fourth century after Christ. At that time there was a flourishing Christianity.... Yet the Roman Empire and the whole system of civilization based upon it were unable to survive. By the beginning of the [fifth] century the collapse had begun, and by the end of the century it was complete. It would seem likely that the same fate awaits the present civilization.... The search for an alternative form of energy may decide the future of our civilization. If the choice of nuclear energy is made, then it may well lead to the destruction of this world, but if an attempt is made to use the natural sources of energy in the sun and water and wind, it may be that civilization will survive.

But whatever the fate of this present world, the real need is to find a way of life which is able to survive all such disasters. In the Roman Empire it was the monastic life which saved the world. It was the monks who fled to the deserts of Egypt, Palestine, and Mesopotamia and founded a way of life based on prayer and work in conditions of the utmost poverty and simplicity who alone survived the collapse of the Roman Empire and whose teaching and example led to the foundation of monasteries all over Europe, in which the basis of a new civilization could be found....

The hope of the future would seem to lie with the small communities...which are springing up all over the world, consisting of men and women, married and single, seeking a new style of life which will be in harmony with nature and with the inner law of the Spirit. These communities cross all barriers of race and religion and are the expression of the urge to go beyond the present economic, political, and religious systems and to open a way to the future.... They can be likened to the monasteries of the Middle Ages, the centers of a ferment which would gradually transform society to make possible a new civilization.

It is to such a community that now, at the end of my life, the Golden String has led me. It was put into my hands while I was still a boy at school and led me first to the discovery of God, then to the discovery of Christ and the Church. I thought then that I had reached the end of my journey, at least in this world, but then it led me to India, and a whole new understanding of the world opened before me. At every stage I have been conscious that it was not I who was leading but that something was leading me. Now it has led me to the point where I have become a sannyasi.[48]

BEYOND THE WORLD
OF APPEARANCES

A sannyasi is one who renounces the world to seek for God, but his renunciation goes far beyond what is ordinarily understood by the "world." A sannyasi is one who renounces not only the world in the biblical sense of the world of sin, the world which today is so clearly set on the path of destruction. A sannyasi renounces the whole world of "signs," of appearances.

The world which is studied by science, the world of politics and economics, the world of social and cultural life, which most people take for reality, is a world of appearances with no ultimate reality. It is all passing away at every moment, and everybody is passing with it. The Church also belongs to this world of "signs." The doctrines and sacraments of the Church are human expressions or signs of the divine reality, which are

likewise destined to pass away. So also Christ himself is the
"sacrament" of God; he is the sign of God's grace and salvation, of God's presence among us, and this sign also will pass,
when the Reality, the thing signified, is revealed. Finally God
himself, insofar as he can be named, whether Yahweh or Al-
lah or simply God, is a sign, a name for the ultimate Truth,
which cannot be named. Thus the sannyasi is called to go beyond all religion, beyond every human institution, beyond every
scripture and creed, till coming to that which every religion and
scripture and ritual signifies but can never name. . . .

Yet when we say that the sannyasi goes beyond religion, this
does not mean that the sannyasi rejects any religion. I have not
felt called to reject anything that I have learned of God or of
Christ or of the Church. To go beyond the sign is not to reject
the sign, but to reach the thing signified. In the language of Saint
Thomas Aquinas, it is to pass from the *sacramentum* to the *res*.
As long as we remain in this world we need these signs, and
the world today cannot survive unless it rediscovers the "signs"
of faith, the "Myth," the "Symbol," in which the knowledge
of reality is enshrined. But equally fatal is to stop at the sign,
to mistake the sign for the ultimate reality. It is this that sets
one religion against another and divides Christians from one
another, from people of other religions and from the rest of
the world. This is essentially idolatry. Whether it is the Bible
or the Church or any dogma or creed, when it is forgotten that
they belong to the world of signs and appearances, to the world
which is passing away, they become idols far more deadly than
any graven image. The sannyasi is one who is called to witness
to this truth of the Reality beyond the signs, to be a sign of that
which is beyond signs.

But when we have said this, we have admitted that the sannyasi, though he may witness to the world beyond signs, yet
himself still belongs to this world. To be true to his vocation
he also must disappear, as Jesus himself, the great sannyasi,

disappeared after the resurrection. He showed himself to his disciples after his resurrection speaking of the kingdom of God,
and then he disappeared. Only when he had gone could the
Spirit come. As he himself said: "It is for your advantage that
I go from you, for if I do not go, the Spirit will not come."
Like the Master, the disciple must disappear. "Unless the grain
of wheat die, it cannot bear fruit." We have to die in order that
we may live. An "ashram" is only a stopping place, in which
a sannyasi may live for a time — or for all "time" — but he
is always journeying beyond time to the eternal reality. So also
every Church, every religion, every human community, is only a
stopping place, a tent which is pitched on this earth by pilgrims
who are on their way to the City of God.

[In *The Golden String*] I had said that the dogmas and sacraments of the Church are the "walls of Jerusalem," the City of
God, and that faith is the gate by which we enter the City. But
when we have entered the City there are no more walls and no
gates, for faith itself must pass away. The City itself is without
boundaries in time or space. In it everything is contained: both
heaven and earth, both fire and air, both sun and moon, and
whatever there is in this world, but no longer divided by sin and
ignorance, no longer limited by space and time, but all realized
in the one Reality, which is pure Consciousness, the consciousness of the eternal Logos and unending bliss, the bliss of the
Holy Spirit, which is love, peace, joy.

There are many people today who think that the kingdom of
God will come in this world, that peace will be established on
earth, that humankind will enjoy lasting happiness. But all this
is an illusion. It is the great *maya* which deceives the world,
which veils the truth. It arises from a refusal to face death.
For those who seek fulfillment in this world, death is an end, a
boundary that cannot be passed. But for those who are willing
to die, death is the gateway to eternal life.

The new world, the world which we seek, is the world of the
resurrection. But this world is already present among us. "The

kingdom of heaven is in your midst." Death is the breakthrough to a new consciousness, a consciousness which is beyond the senses and beyond the mind and opens on the eternal and the infinite. We may only catch glimpses of it now, but it is spreading throughout the world: "The former things have passed away. Behold, I make all things new."[49]

A NEW AGE

With Jesus and the resurrection a new age has dawned. The real world, which he called the kingdom of God, was revealed. Humanity was called to enter the kingdom, to pass beyond space and time, and to enter eternal reality.... [Jesus] said, "I have a baptism to undergo, and what constraint I am under until it is accomplished." He had to go through death in order to enter into the new world, the world of communion with God. We have to go through death with him. It is the only way. This is the challenge that faces the world today. We are passing out of one world, the world of Western domination, and entering a new age in which the logical, rational mind of Greek philosophy and Roman law, the economic and political order, the science and technology of the West, will pass away. Our patriarchal culture is passing away at this present moment.

Something new is emerging. Nobody knows exactly what form it is going to take. It is a moment of trauma, of birth. We are waiting until all the present forms and structures pass away, and we shall see the whole universe in space and time and the whole of humanity, redeemed by Christ, standing in the fullness of reality.[50]

The old is always passing away, and the new is always coming into birth. But we can be insensitive to this, by clinging to the old and thinking, "This is it." Then we stop the movement of creation. Instead, we can allow things to grow and to move, and enter into the new creation. That is what we are challenged to do....

The threat to the very existence of the earth has never been so severe. Many of you may have read *The Dream of the Earth* by Thomas Berry....He points to the terrible tragedy that is being enacted on the planet through technology. We are ruining the earth with pollution of the air and water and the deterioration of the ozone layer which protects us from harmful rays of the sun. The great rain forests, which are a source of life for the entire planet, are rapidly being cut down....That which has taken billions of years to grow is being destroyed in a matter of decades. This is what is happening to our planet.

All these disasters are signs of rebirth. The disaster is coming, but a new creation is coming out of the disaster, from death to resurrection. The people of the earth today are all in trouble. Whole nations are changing their way of life. A system of government that threatened to dominate the world has suddenly dissolved. The situation in the former Soviet Union is one of the most dramatic in history....Many thought that the Soviet Union would eventually control the world, and at times it looked that way. Communism spread beyond Russia to China and to parts of Africa and South America. A nuclear war seemed inevitable, and then, suddenly, the whole thing disintegrated. We are living in a world of tremendous drama, tragedy, and hope.

The Church is also undergoing a crisis, greater perhaps than ever before. The Second Vatican Council was a major breakthrough....A revolution took place in the Catholic Church, which has opened our hearts to a new vision of the Church, which we are still trying to live with. But that was only a beginning. A vast evolution has still to take place. I would say that in the next ten years, more basic changes will occur. We have to see the Holy Spirit working in the world, in the Church, in our lives, transforming us day by day. If we respond to it, then a new age will dawn.[51]

SCIENCE OR WISDOM?

In the ancient world every human activity was in principle a Yoga — a means of union with the divine. Plowing and sowing, spinning and weaving, carpentry and building, dance and song, poetry and philosophy, even war and government, were all seen as integral activities of the whole person, relating the human person to the cosmos and to the cosmic law; hence there was a balance and harmony in life, a balance and harmony always threatened by sin but always preserved in principle. But in the modern world the principle of balance and harmony has been lost....

Modern science — that is, the science which has developed since the Renaissance — is intrinsically defective both in its principles and in its methods. It is defective in principle because it looks upon the material world as an independent reality, and it is defective in its methods because it treats the material world as though it obeyed mechanical laws which are independent of the law of the Spirit. But in reality the material world is a part — and an inferior part — of a greater whole. According to ancient tradition there are three "worlds" — the physical, the psychic, and the spiritual — and these worlds are interdependent as an integrated whole....

This is the root cause of the "disease" of modern civilization. Matter is separated from spirit, body from soul, humankind from nature. Of course, this conflict has been present in the world from the beginning; it is the effect of original sin. But in every culture the principle of integration was preserved. That is why the materialist and the atheist were always regarded as antisocial and antihuman. They deny the principle on which human society rests. This is not to deny that there are laws of matter which can be studied in isolation — the astonishing success of modern science is evidence of this. But these laws have to be related to the psychic laws on which they depend, and these in turn to the ultimate spiritual law. Goethe was one of the few in modern times who was able to conceive a science of this nature. So he wrote, "Perhaps there was a possibility of another method, one which would not tackle nature merely by dissecting and particularizing, but show her at work, and alive, manifesting herself in her wholeness, in every single part of her being." This is a vision of an integral science which has yet to be realized.[52]

The present state of the world is not due to some defect in the use of science and technology, which can be corrected. Western science and technology are based on a false philosophy which has undermined the whole of Western civilization. It is based on the belief, of which Descartes was the spokesman in the seventeenth century, that there is a material world, extended in space and time, independent of human consciousness, and that the human mind can examine this world objectively and so arrive at a knowledge of "reality" which will give him control over the world. This view has now been proved false by science itself, but the old-fashioned view of science and reality still dominates the ordinary person in the West. Marxism is only an extreme form of this illusory view of reality, and the whole of the Western world is more or less subject to it.

There can be little hope therefore that Western science and technology will change their basic character. The only hope lies in a deliberate break with the whole system and an attempt to reconstruct science and technology on a new basis. This will only come when the Western world has undergone a radical change of consciousness — a change which will probably be accompanied by a breakdown of the present system — and has recovered the wisdom of the ancient world, the world not only of Christian Europe but of India and China and Islam. Unfortunately India and China and the Arab world are now exposed to the full force of Western science and technology with all its devastating effects. The new world must therefore be the creation of East and West together, seeking to recover the wisdom which has been lost and to advance into the new age now beginning.[53]

MAHATMA GANDHI'S IDEAL

No one who has lived long in India can fail to be aware of the tremendous problem of poverty in India, which, in spite of all the efforts which have been made since independence, has increased rather than diminished, in the sense that the poor have grown poorer while the rich have grown richer. In regard to this I remain a convinced disciple of Mahatma Gandhi. A great many Christians in India are convinced that a social revolution based on a Marxist analysis of society is the only answer to the needs of India. With this I entirely disagree. To me the fatal defect of Marxism and all forms of socialism is that they take for granted the present industrial system and seek to change the ownership of the means of production of wealth and the method of its distribution but not the actual system of production. But I believe with Gandhi that it is the present system of technology, based on a mechanical system of science, which is the root cause of imbalance in the world today.

In recent years there has been a revolution in Western science as indicated by Fritjof Capra's book *The Tao of Physics* and his more recent book *The Turning Point*. In these books he shows that Western science is moving from a mechanistic model of the universe from which modern technology is derived, to an organic model, a model in which... nature is not dead matter to be exploited by humankind, as has been done in the present system, but a living organism for which humankind is responsible. What is sought today therefore is a new form of technology, which will not seek to dominate and manipulate nature but will work in harmony with nature out of reverence for life....

It is this kind of technology which alone is meaningful in India and the third world and which corresponds with Gandhi's ideal of building up from the villages in which the vast majority of the people of Asia still live. It is true that the Gandhian method has failed in India so far. That is because it cannot compete with the present industrial system. But when this system begins to break down, as it will surely do, it will then be found that the Gandhian method is the only answer to the world's problems. This extends not only to the problems of economics but also to social and political problems. I firmly believe that the peace of the world will never be found as long as the present system prevails. It is only when we have learned reverence for nature that we will learn to be at peace with one another and bring peace to the world.[54]

[Gandhi's] idea of *ahimsa* [nonviolence] is derived from Indian tradition, not only Hindu, but also Jain and Buddhist; it is an ideal which, once formulated some five hundred years before the birth of Christ, has gradually permeated the heart and mind of India. There is no doubt, either, that Gandhi's first acquaintance with *ahimsa* was through the Jain and Hindu traditions of his native Gujerat. But it is no less clear that the reading of the Sermon on the Mount and the writings of Tolstoy transformed this somewhat negative conception into a positive, dynamic force in his life, which he believed was capable of transforming the world....

He believed that moral strength is always greater than physical strength and that [whoever] gives way to violence is morally weak. But such moral strength he believed must be based on a complete freedom from hatred. "It is no nonviolence," he wrote, "if we merely love those who love us. It is nonviolence when we love those who hate us." He had no illusions about the difficulty of this, but he showed in his struggle with the British in India that he was capable of carrying it out in practice.

Again he was convinced that nonviolence was incompatible with fear. "We must give up all external fears. The internal foes we must always fear. We are rightly afraid of animal passion, anger, and the like. External fears cease of their own accord, once we have conquered the enemy in the camp." Thus it is clear that the discipline of nonviolence is one which demands the overcoming of passion in all its forms: fear, anger, hatred, and also lust, for Gandhi believed that *brahmacharya*, that is, chastity, whether in the married or the unmarried, was a necessary condition for a *satyagrahi* [practitioner of nonviolence]. He summed the whole matter up when he said: "Nonviolence implies as complete a self-purification as is humanly possible."

Thus far it might be said that Gandhi was following the Hindu ascetic ideal, only making it of universal application and extending it to people living in the world and exercising their political rights. But there was a further element in his conception of *ahimsa,* which seems to derive from the teaching and example of Christ alone. This was his belief in the efficacy of suffering. "The *satyagrahi,*" he said, "seeks to convert his opponent by sheer force of character and suffering. The purer he is and the more he suffers, the quicker the process." That this view of the mystical value of suffering was derived from the example of Christ he showed clearly when he wrote: "I saw that nations like individuals could only be made through the agony of the cross and in no other way. Joy comes not out of the infliction of pain on others but out of pain voluntarily borne by oneself." We have here, surely, the key to Gandhi's whole doctrine. He had the courage to apply to the struggle for national independence the principle of suffering for justice' sake, which he saw to be the principle of the life and teaching of Christ.

It is this that gives Gandhi's teaching such an immediate relevance to our own problems. For centuries the Church has accepted the principle that violence is a normal way of settling international disputes. Rules have been laid down, not very successfully, to limit the degree of violence which may be used, but few have had the courage to suggest that the principle of suffering for the sake of justice, which was proclaimed in the Sermon on the Mount and exemplified in the passion of Christ, can be applied in the social and political world. This was what Gandhi had the courage to do, and this was the method by which he won independence for India.[55]

MATERIALISM AND
THE ECOLOGICAL CRISIS

There is a general feeling today that we are at the end of an age, an age which began three centuries ago with the discoveries of Galileo and Newton and resulted in the gradual development of a materialist philosophy and a mechanistic model of the universe. This has in the course of time affected our whole society. The present industrial system and modern technology are the direct result of this mechanistic concept of the universe. The whole social, political, and economic system of the West is governed by it, and even art, morality, and religion are affected by it. So we live in a world which came into being in the last three centuries, and has come to a head only in the last century.

The basic principle of this world is its materialistic philosophy. This materialism is explicit in Marxism, but it is implicit practically everywhere, and it governs people's attitudes of mind and behavior. Its basic principle is reductionism: it is the reduction of everything to certain material principles and to its material base. To take a simple example, all music can be reduced to vibrations on strings or in a pipe, mere vibrations in the air, and those vibrations may then be treated as what music is, without concern for any other value which belongs to it. Fritjof Capra has shown convincingly in *The Turning Point* (1982) how this mechanistic system has come to dominate every aspect of science and of practical life today.[56]

This is a drastic system by which everything is reduced to the material level, and it has had extraordinary success. Scientifically it has led to great discoveries being made, and it has undoubtedly produced an impressive system of technology. On a social scale it has produced states with tremendous power building up influence all over the world. But at the same time it is gradually producing inevitable evil effects, rapidly exhausting material resources, polluting the environment, and leading to the build-up of armaments which threatens to lead to a nuclear war capable of destroying our entire civilization and the whole planet. All this is the result of three centuries of materialism building up to its height in the first part of this century.

In the second part of this century we have begun to discover what has been taking place and in what we are involved, and a new movement has begun which is the opposite of all this. We are beginning now to be able to replace the mechanistic system and the mechanistic model of the universe with an organic model. This is the beginning of a return to the traditional wisdom, the wisdom by which human beings have lived over thousands and thousands of years, and with which the great societies of the past have been built up. In this ancient, traditional wisdom the order of the universe is seen always to be threefold, consisting not only of a physical dimension but also of a psychological and a spiritual world. The three worlds were always seen as interrelated and interdependent. This understanding of the three orders of being and of their interdependence is what is known as the perennial philosophy.[57]

CATASTROPHE OR RENEWAL?

It is possible that the transition from a mechanistic to an organic society will come about gradually, without too much conflict. But it is more likely that there will be a general catastrophe, as the economic, social, and political structures of the present civilization break down. We must remember — and this is important — that the conflicts of the present world do not derive merely from human failings and miscalculations. There has been a reversal of human values, a spiritual breakdown, which has brought into play forces beyond the material and the human. The present crisis has been prepared by the whole system of science and philosophy, affecting religion and leading to atheism. This is a systematic development where the previous spiritual values have been broken down and the materialistic system discussed earlier has prevailed. This has released forces beyond the material and the human. If a nuclear war takes place, it will not be because anyone desires it but because people are being driven by forces of the unconscious which they cannot control. As Saint Paul says, "We are not contending with flesh and blood, but against the principalities, against the powers, against the world rulers of this present darkness." When the truth of the transcendent order of reality is rejected, we do not remain neutral. We become exposed to the hostile forces of the subtle world of which we have been speaking, forces which work in the unconscious and bring destruction upon humankind. Western Europe rejected the perennial philosophy at the Renaissance and has been led step by step to the materialistic philosophy which rejects fundamental human values and exposes humankind to the contrary forces at work in the universe. The only way of recovery is to rediscover the perennial philosophy, the traditional wisdom, which is found in all ancient religions and especially in the great religions of the world. But those religions have in turn become fossilized and have each to be renewed, not only in themselves but also in relation to one another, so that a cosmic, universal religion can emerge, in which the essential values of Christian religion will be preserved in living relationship with the other religious traditions of the world. This is a task for the coming centuries as the present world order breaks down and a new world order emerges from the ashes of the old.[58]

5

Final Unity

Bede Griffiths was a person of unity. All his life was aimed at bringing together that which the religions had divided and which science and secular humanism had not succeeded in uniting. He pursued this aim through a series of personal choices which determined the course of his long life.

He came to India to find the other half of his soul. But neither in his early years there nor in the last phase of his life was his search aimed at a merely personal fulfillment. Although he founded no monasteries or intentional communities, he created communion among people who otherwise would have proceeded forever on divergent paths.

Although he recognized the divisive effects of religious conflicts in European and human history in general, he remained convinced that unity was a religious problem and that the meeting of the religions was an essential contribution to its solution.

Father Bede also spoke of "one religion"; this religion was for him already in existence, and he found it — veiled, perhaps, even disfigured in some of its historical moments — in the Christianity which he had embraced at the end of his university studies and which he never came anywhere near to renouncing. Every question he raised and every criticism he voiced was expressed from within the great catholic communion of believers in the Christ mystery. Many of these questions and criticisms were published in the form of letters to the British Catholic periodical The Tablet. *Perhaps another anthology will gather up these articles and make them available to the readers of this book. They will show the strong sense of belonging which permeated even his objections to the slow pace of Church reform or to ecclesiastical backtracking on ecumenism.*

The source of unity, or, better yet, the personification of unity, is Jesus Christ. However, the Christ of Father Bede's faith was nothing like the Christ-Emperor whom some believers imagine sallying forth as a conqueror or a vindicator. Christ does not recapture but recapitulates the history of humanity by incarnating human destiny. In The Golden String, *Bede saw Christ fulfilling the ancient myths, and he returned time and again to this doctrine of "fulfillment" in the course of his earlier writings about the religions in general and Hinduism in particular.*

In his later writings, the favorite formula was "complementarity," and the sense of the word implies the nuptial archetype: only with the union of "both halves" of the human soul will the one religion emerge. Although Father Bede quoted biblical and medieval Christian sources in elaborating this formula, he often expressed the opinion that the Bible contained a hard core of "dualism" which had to be broken down through contact with India and the Far East. Sometimes he seemed to affirm that what he called "Semitic monotheism" could never enter into the harmony of a universal wisdom and a universal religion. On the other hand, he found that the Jewish and Christian mystics went well beyond a monotheistic dualism of a God who stands over against the cosmos.

Father Bede found the remedy for ethical and metaphysical dualism (including not only the Bible but also Plato and Descartes) in the trinitarian mystery of the Christian tradition. Here he simply continued the idea elaborated first by Jules Monchanin and Henri Le Saux. The understanding of God as "subsistent relations," as a communion in love, was not only an

intellectual theory for Bede Griffiths. It was the substance of his
personal experience and revealed to him the image of human
and religious unity.

THE MEETING OF RELIGIONS

The religions of the world are meeting today in a way they
have never done before. Each religion grew up in a particular
cultural setting, Hinduism and Buddhism in India, Taoism and
Confucianism in China, Judaism and Christianity in Palestine,
Islam in Arabia. But in the course of time each religion grew
and extended its influence. Hinduism remained largely confined
to India, but the meeting of Aryan people from the north with
the Dravidian and other indigenous people from other parts led
to a continuous growth and enrichment of their religion, which
gave it a universal character. Likewise the two opposite traditions of Taoism and Confucianism in China led to the growth
of a profound, universal wisdom which united the whole of
China. Buddhism, beginning in India, spread to Sri Lanka,
Burma, Thailand, and Vietnam, and then with the growth of
Mahayana doctrine to Tibet, Korea, China, and Japan. Judaism
and Christianity both began in Palestine, but Judaism spread in
the "Diaspora" over the Middle East and Europe and North Africa and eventually the whole world. Christianity spread first of
all westward over the Roman Empire and eastward over Syria,
Mesopotamia, and Persia and as far as India and China, while
in the West it became the dominant religion of Europe and
America. Islam, beginning in Arabia, spread westward to North
Africa as far as Spain and eastward over Syria, Turkey, and Iraq
to Iran, India, and Indonesia.

With this geographical extension there took place an extraordinary development of doctrine. The primitive Vedic mythology
developed in Yoga, Vedanta, and Tantra into an elaborate system of mystical philosophy, moral discipline, and an immense,

ritualistic religion. The earlier Buddhist doctrine, with its limited view of individual salvation in Nirvana, evolved into the
Mahayana doctrine of universal salvation, with the Bodhisattva
making a vow not to enter Nirvana until every living being
has been saved. Judaism developed in the Talmud an elaborate system of law, and later in the Qabbalah a subtle, mystical
doctrine. Christianity, under the influence of Greek philosophy
and Roman law, developed a vast system of ritual and doctrine
which shaped the history of Europe and America and extended
to the European colonies of Asia and Africa. Most remarkable
of all, in some ways, the primitive religion of the Quran, from
its contact with the civilization of Syria, Egypt, Iraq, and Iran,
developed a sophisticated culture, and by absorbing the philosophy of Plato and Aristotle produced its own unique philosophy
and theology.

But in spite of this extraordinary expansion of each religion,
it is only today that these different religious traditions are beginning to mix freely all over the world and are seeking to relate
to one another, not in terms of rivalry and conflict, but in terms
of dialogue and mutual respect. One of the greatest needs of
humanity today is to transcend the cultural limitations of the
great religions and to find a wisdom, a philosophy, which can
reconcile their differences and reveal the unity which underlies
all their diversities. This has been called the "perennial philosophy," the eternal wisdom which has been revealed in a different
way in each religion.

The perennial philosophy stems from a crucial period in
human history in the middle of the first millennium before
Christ. It was then that a breakthrough was made beyond the
cultural limitations of ancient religion to the experience of ultimate reality. This reality, which has no proper name, since it
transcends the mind and cannot be expressed in words, was
called Brahman and Atman (the Spirit) in Hinduism, Nirvana
and Sunyata (the Void) in Buddhism, Tao (the Way) in China,
Being (*to on*) in Greece, and Yahweh ("I am") in Israel, but all

these are but words which point to an inexpressible mystery, in which the ultimate meaning of the universe is to be found, but which no human word or thought can express. It is this which is the goal of all human striving, the truth which all science and philosophy seeks to fathom, the bliss in which all human love is fulfilled. . . .

This philosophy, which prevailed in almost all parts of the world until the fifteenth century, was rejected in Europe in the sixteenth century, and a new system of philosophy based on the findings of Western science has taken its place. But the philosophy of Western science itself has now begun to disintegrate as a result of the new scientific developments in relativity and quantum physics. Consequently, the world today is left with no basic philosophy which can give meaning to life, and we are in danger of losing all sense of meaning and purpose in human existence. When to this is added the devastating effect of Western technology on the ecology of the planet, which threatens to destroy the world on which we depend for our very existence, it can be seen that the need of a philosophy, a universal wisdom which can unify humanity and enable us to face the problems created by Western science and technology, has become the greatest need of humanity today. The religions of the world cannot by themselves answer this need. They are themselves today part of the problem of a divided world. The different world religions — Hinduism, Buddhism, Judaism, Christianity, and Islam — have themselves to recover the ancient wisdom which they have inherited, and this has now to be interpreted in the light of the knowledge of the world which Western science has given us.[59]

ONE RELIGION

According to the Letter to the Colossians, in Christ "all things were created, in heaven and on earth . . . all were created through him and for him." This is a truly cosmic vision embracing the whole created world, which we now know to be an integrated whole, and this forms a body, a living organism, which is capable of embracing all humanity. We have therefore the conception of a universal community capable of embodying the universal wisdom and uniting all humanity in one body, one living whole, in which the "fullness," the whole, of the Godhead dwells....

Each religion has to undergo a death and resurrection — a death to its historical and cultural limitations and a resurrection to a new life in the Spirit, which would embody the traditions of the universal wisdom in a way which responds to the need of humanity today. No doubt we are all very far from realizing this unity, but as the different religions of the world meet today, we are discovering our common heritage and becoming aware of the unity which binds together the whole human race and makes it aware of its responsibility for the whole created universe. The concept of one world, one human race, and one religion based on the universal wisdom has acquired a new significance, as a way to escape from the disastrous conflicts which are dividing the world today.[60]

Each religion must learn to discern its essential truth and to reject its cultural and historical limitations. This may be a painful experience, a rejection of innumerable elements in religion which have grown up with the cultural and historical development of a religion and have often been identified with the religion itself. Yet this seems to be the only path open to humanity today. What stands in the way is the dominant mentality of the Western world. This is the hour of trial for "Western man." Will he continue to build up his scientific world with nuclear power leading to the devastation of the earth, or will he learn to repent, to turn back, to rediscover the source of life, the wisdom of Mother Earth, which is also the wisdom of the East?[61]

At no time in history has the world been nearer to destruction than it is at the present moment. There are forces present in the world which are capable of destroying all life on this planet, and those who control these forces are themselves beyond control. It may be that the Western world will change, or at least a sufficient number will be there to initiate a change, to undergo a *metanoia,* a change of heart, and set the world on another course, bringing about the marriage of East and West. But there can be no finality even in this. Our destiny is not in this world, and we have to be prepared to go beyond death. We have to die to this world and everything in it, that is, everything that changes and passes in this world, to find the reality which does not change or pass. Above all, we have to go beyond words and images and concepts. No imaginative vision or conceptual framework is adequate to the great reality. When Christ will appear in glory, it will not be in any earthly form or in any manner we can conceive. "For now we see in a mirror dimly, but then face to face"; and we shall only "appear in glory" when we have died to ourselves and become a "new creation." Then alone shall we encounter the fullness of truth and reality which is also the fullness of wisdom and knowledge and the fullness of bliss and love. Then only will the final marriage take place, of East and West, of man and woman, of matter and mind, of time and eternity.[62]

CHRIST THE SOURCE

The Second Vatican Council said that "the Church rejects nothing that is true and holy in other religions." There is truth and holiness in all genuine religion. Their knowledge and understanding is often very imperfect, but it can grow. The Christian mission is to help other people to grow, but also to learn from them so that our Christian faith grows too. It has been our experience in the ashram that the more we open ourselves to the other religions, to Hinduism in particular, the deeper our Christian faith grows. Our aim is the deepening of our own faith, which then becomes more open to others.

This is not easy, and everybody has to answer the question for themselves. I like the illustration of fingers and the palm of the hand. The fingers represent Buddhism, Hinduism, Islam, Judaism, and [the thumb represents] Christianity. Buddhism is miles from Christianity, and each has its own position. If you try to mix them, taking a bit of Hinduism or Buddhism and adding it to Christianity, that is syncretism. But if you go deeply into any one tradition, you converge on a center, and there you see how we all come forth from a common root. And you find how we meet people on the deeper level of their faith, in the profound unity behind all our differences.

Father [Jules] Monchanin...saw how we had to meet the Hindus at the source of their religion in the Upanishads, the Vedas, the Gita. In Christianity the source is in the New Testament, the early Fathers, and the first monks. But if you look to the seventeenth or eighteenth century, it is very difficult to meet. It is in the source we discovery unity. Our spiritual journey today is to go back to the source of all religions. Christ is ultimately the source of all religion. He is behind it all.[63]

He is called the "Second Adam." Adam is humanity which falls away from God and is involved in sin, suffering, and death. Jesus is the new Adam who reconciles humanity with God. One of the early Church councils said there is no human being whose nature is not redeemed by Christ. We are all born into a common human nature which is both fallen and redeemed. The grace of Christ is present in some way to every human being from the beginning to the end. Normally it comes through their traditional religion....

In India the Christians used to look at the Hindus and see pagans under the power of the devil, from which they must be rescued. But now we try to see that Christ is already present. Our call is to draw out that presence of Christ, to make them realize it more and more fully. In India sometimes you meet the most Christlike people among Hindus, and there is no doubt that the Presence is there.[64]

Of course, learning from each other carries the danger of syncretism. Most Hindus I know are syncretists; they think it is all the same whether you believe in Jesus, Krishna, Rama, or Buddha. We are not syncretists like that, but we do believe that each religion has its own, unique value and insights which we need to share with one another. We have our own unique way through revelation in Christ and through the Church. We try to share that with others, but we recognize too that God has revealed himself in other ways to other people, and so we try to recognize their values. Respect for other people's religion and culture is the crucial thing, and I think, on the whole, this is the way the Church is moving today.[65]

FULFILLMENT IN CHRIST

Christ came to recapitulate all the stages of human history, to sum up in himself the destiny of humankind. It was no accident he was born in a cave. He traveled the whole of that long, difficult, and laborious path by which we have to return to the Father. He went down like Aeneas into the underworld; he passed through death into life; he ascended above this world of space and time into the divine presence.

But Christ did not open this path for himself alone. On the day before he was to die, he instituted a rite by which his disciples might be able to follow him on the same path by which he had traveled. He took bread and wine, the symbols of sacrifice throughout the ancient world, and made them the sacramental means by which his disciples might share in the mystery of his death and enter into new life with him.

It is here in the sacrifice, accomplished once in time on the Cross and renewed sacramentally day by day under the symbols of bread and wine, that all religion finds its fulfillment.... For what was it that took place in the interior darkness of the cave? There can be no doubt of the answer; it is the mystery of sacrifice. At the center of all religion in the holy place, where the encounter with the divine mystery is to take place, stands the altar of sacrifice.

And what is sacrifice? To sacrifice is literally to "make a thing sacred"; it is to take something out of common use and to make it over to God. It is a symbolic act by which we recognize that everything in this world derives from another order of being and seek to enter into communion with that other world. But the outward thing which is sacrificed can never be more than a sign of inward offering; what we desire has to take place in the center of our own being, in the darkness of the interior where alone we can encounter the God who is hidden in the depths of the soul. We have to pass beyond all the images of the senses, beyond all the concepts of the mind, beyond ourselves, if we are really to find God.

But this is precisely what of ourselves we can never do. We have become separated from the center of our being, we have lost the thread in the maze. We wander endlessly exploring the mouth of the cave, living in a world of shadows. Never has humankind experienced more appallingly than at the present day this sense of separation from reality; the world has become a nightmare from which there seems to be no escape.

Where then is the clue to the center? Where is the Golden String to be found? The Golden String is Christ; he is the clue to the center. The sacrifice of Christ is the central event of human history; it is the event which alone gives meaning to life. It was in the Resurrection of Christ that the illusion of this world was shattered, and humankind was set free from the bondage of space and time.[66]

FINAL UNITY

In the Hindu revelation, the ultimate reality is *Sat-cit-ananda* — "Being, Knowledge, Bliss." The search is for that ultimate Being, that ultimate Reality — *sat*. And that Being and Reality is conscious; it is *cit,* "Consciousness," a conscious awareness of infinite and eternal Being. And the consciousness of that eternal Being is Bliss, *ananda,* "pure joy." That is the goal of Hinduism — to reach that *Saccidananda,* and that *Saccidananda* is pure oneness, One without a second.

In the Gospel there is a further depth revealed. In the ultimate reality there is revealed not merely an identity, but a communion. The final Christian revelation is that the Godhead itself, the ultimate reality, is a communion of persons, a communion of persons in love, and that gives a further dimension to our understanding of reality. The Hindu believes that God is love, in a sense, and that you can love God, but not that the Godhead itself is love. There cannot be love without two. If God is a pure monad, as he is in Islam, as he tends to be in Hinduism, he cannot be love in himself. But in the Christian concept, the Godhead itself is love, is a communion of love. There is a distinction within the Godhead itself, distinction beyond our comprehension which we crudely express in terms of person and relation. These are human terms pointing to the reality. The reality is that God is love, that there is something which corresponds to personal communion in love in the Godhead, and we are called to share in that communion of love.

So also, in the mystical body of Christ which embraces all redeemed humanity, we do not disappear in the Godhead, but we discover a personal relationship of love. Each person is fulfilled and is open to the other person; it is an intercommunion of love in which each embraces the other and all are embraced in God.

In the *Paradiso* in Dante's *Divine Comedy* there is a poetic description which goes as far as human intelligence can toward depicting this mystery of the Trinity as love. And that is what we are called to experience — this communion of love in the mystical body of Christ which embraces the whole creation. All the beauty of the creation is present there for our joy and our thanksgiving. The whole of redeemed humanity is there, and each of us, according to our capacity, is able to go out in love to others and to be embraced in love by others. All creation and all humanity are taken up into this infinite, incomprehensible, inexpressible Being of God, in whom — though we can never understand or comprehend him — we know that there is this communion of charity, this communion of love. Jesus expresses it marvelously in the Gospel of Saint John when he prays, "That they may be one, as thou, Father, in me and I in thee, that they may be one in us." That is Christian *advaita*. We are one with one another and one with Christ; we are one in this mystery of the Godhead, and I do not think we can go beyond that. This would be an example of how to relate the cosmic revelation to the Christian revelation. We are all engaged in this task, and it is not something fully accomplished; it is that to which we are moving.[67]

We need today to take very seriously the view of humanity as one body, one organic whole, [the view] of the Adam who is in all humanity. Saint Thomas Aquinas, in a beautiful phrase, said, "Omnes homines, unus homo" (All people are one person). We are all members of that one . . . who fell and became divided in conflict and confusion. Jesus restored humanity, not only Jews or Christians or any particular group, to that oneness. In the new Adam the human race becomes conscious of its fundamental unity and of its unity with the cosmos. . . .

Both types of awareness have come to us today, seeing humanity as a whole and seeing humanity as a part of the cosmic whole. We are all part of this planet, united by it and growing and living from it. We are all parts of each other, growing through contact with one another as one organic whole. We are recovering that unity beyond duality. Humanity had to go through dualism, to learn the difference between right and wrong, good and evil, truth and error. It is necessary to go through that stage of separating and dividing, but then you have to transcend it. The Old Testament generally reflects this duality: it was always the Israelites who were the holy people, and outside were the gentiles who were to be rejected. The good were to be separate, and the evil condemned. This dualism runs through all the Jewish tradition.

Jesus came from that Jewish tradition and often uses its language of rejection and condemnation. Yet all the time he was going beyond it and taking us to the point where we transcend all dualities. This is marvelously expressed in Saint John's Gospel: "May they all be one.... " Here Jesus shows that he is totally one with the Father, and yet he is not the Father. It is a nondual relationship. It is not one, and it is not two. When two people unite in love, they become one and yet keep their distinctiveness. Jesus and the Father had this total communion in love, and he asks us to become one with him as he is one with the Father: total oneness in the nondual Being of the Godhead. It is the Christian calling to recover this unity. In India *advaita* [the philosophy of nondualism] has many forms; some are not at all satisfactory, but the idea of *advaita,* nonduality, is fundamental to Christian understanding today.

Christianity came out of a tradition of moral dualism. It then passed into the Greco-Roman culture, which was based on a metaphysical dualism. But today it is meeting the religions of Asia, and we are beginning to discover the principle of nonduality. The rational mind demands that everything be one or two, while nonduality, which is beyond the rational, affirms a relationship which is not one and not two. It is only through meditation that we get beyond this duality. We are being called to recover unity beyond duality as our birthright, and it is this alone which can answer the deepest needs of the world today.

[In my book *Universal Wisdom*] I try to show that every religion — Hinduism, Buddhism, Taoism, Islam, Judaism, and Christianity — has a dualistic element as its starting point, but then moves into this nondualism.... Every religion goes beyond dualism through its mystical tradition. This is our calling and our hope.

Meditation is the only way to go beyond dualism. As long as you think rationally, you will have a dualistic attitude. But when you stop the mind, you discover the unifying principle behind everything.... Everywhere people are meeting together, discovering this need and responding to it in the different ways of meditation. We are being called to open our hearts to the nondual mystery which is the mystery of love revealed in the Trinity.

In the doctrine of the Trinity, the ultimate Reality is seen as Being in relationship, or Being in love. The ultimate Reality is not a solitary person nor an impersonal Absolute. It is a communion of persons in love. Every being seeks to express and communicate itself. In the human being, the body is one means by which we express ourselves and communicate with others. But the highest expression of our being is the mind. It is through the mind that we find words to express and communicate ourselves. In the Godhead as conceived by the Christian tradition, the Word of God is the expression of the mind of God. It is the self-manifestation of the eternal Wisdom; and the Spirit of God, the Holy Spirit, is the self-communication of the eternal Being, infinite love, which is manifested in the whole of creation and comes to a head in the person of Jesus Christ. It is the experience of this eternal Wisdom, communicated in the love of the Holy Spirit, that our meditation should lead us.[68]

THE COMMUNION OF LOVE

The divine Wisdom, or the ultimate Truth, is known not only by words written in a book or by philosophy enshrined in doctrine, but in the "flesh," that is, in the actual, concrete conditions of human existence. Jesus was crucified "under Pontius Pilate" at a particular time and place and in a particular historic situation. On the other hand, the Fourth Gospel reveals above all the intimate relation between Jesus and God. The earliest tradition does not speak of Jesus as God: that was a later theological development.... Jesus himself in the Fourth Gospel constantly speaks of himself in relation to God and refers everything he says and does to its source in the "Father." This is the particular Christian revelation, not that Jesus was God, as Rama and Krishna can be said to be God, but that he stood in a unique relation to God as Son to the Father.

It is significant that Muhammad in the Quran insisted that God had no son. This would have undermined the solitary isolation of the monotheistic God in whom he believed. By calling himself Son, Jesus recognized relationship in God, in the ultimate Truth and Reality. God in this understanding is not a solitary Monad. The Godhead, the divine being itself, is constituted by relationship. But this means not only that Jesus is the Son of God but that all humanity in Jesus is brought into this relationship with God. Creation itself, according to Thomas Aquinas, is a relation to God. It has no existence in itself but exists only in relation to God. In Jesus the whole creation and the whole of humanity are brought into this living relationship which Jesus shares with the Father. We are made "partakers of the divine nature." It is this that Semitic monotheism refuses to recognize, but the whole tradition of the universal wisdom recognizes this intimate relation between God and humanity, between God and creation. The world is not divided; there is no separation between God and the world. Relationship is not identity. Jesus is not identical with the Father. This is not monism or dualism but "nondualism" (*advaita*), which is a transcendent relationship which cannot properly be expressed in human terms.

If Jesus is one with the Father, with God, in this unique relationship, so also are those who respond to this call. The Word which "became flesh" in Jesus "enlightens everyone who comes into the world." This Word is the Light, the Truth, the Word of Guru Nanak, the Name which is above every name, the Guru within to whom every external guru bears witness. When Jesus departed from his disciples he sent the Holy Spirit to be with them forever. The Holy Spirit is the indwelling presence of God, the source of all wisdom, truth, and goodness. Above all it is the Love which created and sustains the world, which is revealed not as a person standing over against the world, but as the Communion of Love which embraces all humanity and all creation and is the Wisdom which orders the universe, for Wisdom is Knowledge by love.[69]

Sources

In this anthology, we draw only on full-length books by Bede Griffiths; although his many published articles are a rich source for his thought and experience, most of their contents were later included, rewritten or as originally published, in his books. We quote the following:

Christ in India: Essays towards a Hindu-Christian Dialogue. Springfield, Ill.: Templegate Publishers, (1965) 1984.

The Cosmic Revelation: The Hindu Way to God. Springfield, Ill.: Templegate Publishers, 1983.

The Golden String. Springfield, Ill.: Templegate Publishers, (1954) 1980.

The Marriage of East and West: A Sequel to The Golden String. Springfield, Ill.: Templegate Publishers, 1982.

The Mystery Beyond: On Retreat with Bede Griffiths. London: Medio Media/Arthur James, 1997.

The New Creation in Christ: Christian Meditation and Community, ed. Robert Kiely and Lawrence Freeman, O.S.B. London: Darton, Longman and Todd, 1992; Springfield, Ill.: Templegate Publishers, 1994.

A New Vision of Reality: Western Science, Eastern Mysticism, and Christian Faith. Springfield, Ill.: Templegate Publishers, (1989) 1992.

Return to the Center. Springfield, Ill.: Templegate Publishers, 1976.

River of Compassion. Springfield, Ill.: Templegate Publishers, (1987) 1994 (forthcoming from Templegate Pulishers).

Universal Wisdom: A Journey through the Sacred Wisdom of the World. San Francisco: HarperSanFrancisco, 1994 (forthcoming from Templegate Pulishers).

Vedanta and Christian Faith. Los Angeles: Dawn Horse Press, 1973.

1. A Vision of Nature

1. *The Golden String,* 9–10.
2. *The Golden String,* 129–30.
3. *The Golden String,* 185.
4. *The Golden String,* 187.

5. *The Golden String*, 180–83.
6. *The Marriage of East and West*, 46–47.
7. *Christ in India*, 20–22.
8. *The Marriage of East and West*, 13–15.
9. *Return to the Center*, 9–12.
10. *Return to the Center*, 34–36.

2. The Challenge of Hinduism

11. *Christ in India*, 9–11.
12. *Christ in India*, 16.
13. *Christ in India*, 19–20.
14. *Christ in India*, 22–23.
15. *Christ in India*, 41–42.
16. *Christ in India*, 62–64.
17. *A New Vision of Reality*, 95.
18. *The Marriage of East and West*, 23–24.
19. *A New Vision of Reality*, 25–26.
20. *The Marriage of East and West*, 47–48.
21. *The Cosmic Revelation*, 37–39.
22. *A New Vision of Reality*, 52–55.
23. *Vedanta and Christian Faith*, 10–14.
24. *The Cosmic Revelation*, 114.
25. *The Cosmic Revelation*, 14–16.
26. *The Cosmic Revelation*, 16.
27. *The Cosmic Revelation*, 112–14.
28. *Christ in India*, 46–47.
29. *The Cosmic Revelation*, 118–19.
30. *Return to the Center*, 84.
31. *The Cosmic Revelation*, 126–28.
32. *River of Compassion*, 64–65.
33. *River of Compassion*, 266–67.
34. *River of Compassion*, 66–69.

3. Awakening to the Feminine

35. *A New Vision of Reality*, 102–4.
36. *The Marriage of East and West*, 120–21.
37. *The Marriage of East and West*, 9–10.
38. *A New Vision of Reality*, 93–94.
39. *Universal Wisdom*, 40–41.
40. *The Marriage of East and West*, 191–94.

41. *The Marriage of East and West*, 129–31.
42. *River of Compassion*, 7.
43. *Return to the Center*, 136–39.
44. *Vedanta and Christian Faith*, 74–75.
45. *The Marriage of East and West*, 150–52.

4. A New Age

46. *The Marriage of East and West*, 7.
47. *The Golden String*, 3–4.
48. *The Marriage of East and West*, 39–41.
49. *The Marriage of East and West*, 42–45.
50. *A New Vision of Reality*, 76–77.
51. *A New Vision of Reality*, 79–80.
52. *Return to the Center*, 93–95.
53. *The Golden String*, 7–8.
54. *Christ in India*, 7–8.
55. *Christ in India*, 144–46.
56. *A New Vision of Reality*, 276.
57. *A New Vision of Reality*, 278.
58. *A New Vision of Reality*, 295–96.

5. Final Unity

59. *Universal Wisdom*, 7–8.
60. *Universal Wisdom*, 42–43.
61. *The Marriage of East and West*, 200.
62. *The Marriage of East and West*, 203–4.
63. *A New Vision of Reality*, 95–97.
64. *A New Vision of Reality*, 99–100.
65. *A New Vision of Reality*, 106.
66. *The Golden String*, 183–84.
67. *The Cosmic Revelation*, 130–31.
68. *A New Vision of Reality*, 48–51.
69. *Universal Wisdom*, 430–31.